Alternative
Shakespeare
Auditions
for Men

Simon Dunmore

A & C Black • London
Theatre Arts Books/Routledge • New York

First published 1997
A & C Black (Publishers) Limited
35 Bedford Row, London WC1R 4JH

ISBN 0–7136–4757–4

A CIP catalogue record for this book is
available from the British Library.

Published in the USA in 1998 by
Theatre Arts Books/Routledge
29 West 35 Street, New York, NY 10001

ISBN 0–87830–075–9

CIP catalog record available at the Library of Congress.

Printed and bound in Great Britain by
Redwood Books, Trowbridge, Wiltshire

Contents

Introduction

Shakespeare is demanded for audition a lot of the time. Unfortunately for auditioners, auditionees tend to choose from a very limited collection of characters and speeches; unfortunately for auditionees, they have to perform those well-known speeches exceptionally well to succeed amongst the incredible competition. Experienced auditioners will have already seen a brilliant Hamlet, Iago and Cassius, to mention but a few, against which we inevitably compare yours. If you use one of the well-known speeches at audition, unless you manage to hit that magic peak of performance, you are on an inevitable slope to failure.

Why do people stick to these popular speeches? I'm convinced that it's largely because they cannot face the idea of getting their heads round unfamiliar plays and characters written in obscure language. It's easier if you already have some idea of the character and play – from studying it at school, seeing a stage production or a film version. I estimate that nearly fifty per cent of *The Complete Works* are rarely performed. There is, sitting there unregarded, a great wealth of material from which the auditionee can draw. Why are they 'rarely performed'? Often because they aren't as good as the famous plays, but they do contain material which is on a par with the greatest moments in Shakespeare. Sometimes, they are 'rarely performed' because the language is especially difficult (*Love's Labour's Lost*, for instance), or because the historical knowledge required to follow the plot is too much for a modern audience (the *Henry VI* plays, for instance), or because the stories on which the plays are based are no longer part of our common culture (*Troilus and Cressida*, for instance). Shakespeare's audiences would not only have understood the jokes and topical references, but also would have had a working knowledge of their recent kings; Greek and Roman history, classical mythology, religious practices, and the Bible would all be much more familiar to them than they are to us now.

Even the well-known plays have lesser known, but not necessarily less interesting, characters in them. For instance, Petruchio from *The Taming of the Shrew* is very popular audition fare, but in this same play is also the relatively unknown Biondello. He is not involved in much of the action of the play, but he has big enough snippet for the auditionee.

Introduction

The other fundamental problem for the auditionee is length. Most people don't realise that fourteen or fifteen lines of verse is often perfectly sufficient (providing it also conforms to the other parameters mentioned in the 'Auditioning Shakespeare' chapter). Just because the famous speeches go on for twice or three times this length it doesn't mean that they mark an 'industry standard'.

I know that it is difficult for women to find 'original' Shakespeare speeches, but I'm afraid the vast majority of men choose from only about thirty different characters from the hundreds available. There are plenty of less obviously important to the plot, but just as well written, men with sufficiently long speeches. You can also look at suitable dialogue and edit it to make a single speech (there are several such in this book). Some people believe the idea of editing Shakespeare is tantamount to sacrilege. I think that this is ridiculous because there is no such thing as a definitive Shakespeare text (this is true for the vast majority of plays; most playwrights have alternative versions to what arrives in print) and also in doing an audition you are performing a mini-play separated from the whole work and it therefore will lose some of the constraints that tied it in its original context. On the other hand editing dialogue is not necessarily simply cutting out the other person's lines. It requires time, thought and trying out to see whether or not it works.

Another thorny problem is punctuation. I largely worked from five different editions of each play and in my researches to date I have not yet found any sustained section of speech which is punctuated the same way in any two given editions. I have tried to rethink the punctuation to suit the modern actor, and I have a pious hope that Shakespeare might largely have approved of what I've done – after all he was working with actors, not academics. There are a number of instances where some words vary between editions, and where there is an important alternative I have mentioned it in the notes.

Line numbering also varies, so I have chosen to number each speech from one. There are only a few instances where this is true of the speech in the play.

I have written notes on everything that might be obscure, but not following the dictates of any one academic editor. You will find I disagree with them all in a few instances. I also looked up every unfamiliar or obscure word in the *Oxford English Dictionary*, which was incredibly useful in illuminating the language. Overall I have tried to help you understand the details of each speech in order to perform it, rather than to write essays about it.

I have also included a short character description for each speech. These are meant to help kick you off in the task of reading the whole play. They are inevitably sketchy and only give the basics leading up to the moment of the speech. I cannot stress too much the fact that there is no substitute for reading and absorbing the whole play.

This book contains just fifty speeches which are rarely, if ever, used in audition. There are plenty more to find if you look hard enough.

Finally, I would like to thank all those who helped me by work-shopping all these speeches before they were committed to print: Fayyaz Ahmed, Phillip Hoffman, Cameron Jack, Matthew Storey and Robert Wilfort; my mother, Alison Dunmore, for supplying me with tit-bits from her decades of watching Shakespeare in perfor-mance, and my wife, Maev Alexander, for her detailed and incisive comments on everything.

Male Characters and Speeches Too Often Used for Audition

Hamlet (*Hamlet*)
Hotspur (*Henry IV, part 1*)
Prince Hal, later Henry V (*Henry IV, parts 1 & 2 and Henry V*)
Chorus (*Henry V*) – The opening speech, 'O for a muse of fire...'
Brutus (*Julius Caesar*)
Cassius (*Julius Caesar*)
Mark Antony (*Julius Caesar*)
Marullus (*Julius Caesar*)
Philip the Bastard (*King John*)
Edgar (*King Lear*)
Edmund (*King Lear*)
Macbeth (*Macbeth*)
Angelo (*Measure for Measure*)
Lancelot Gobbo (*The Merchant of Venice*)
Shylock (*The Merchant of Venice*)
Bottom (*A Midsummer Night's Dream*)
Egeus (*A Midsummer Night's Dream*)
Oberon (*A Midsummer Night's Dream*)
Puck (*A Midsummer Night's Dream*)
Benedick (*Much Ado About Nothing*)
Iago (*Othello*)
Othello (*Othello*)
Richard II (*Richard II*)
Clarence (*Richard III*)
Richard III (*Richard III*)
Mercutio (*Romeo and Juliet*)
Romeo (*Romeo and Juliet*)
Petruchio (*The Taming of the Shrew*)
Trinculo (*The Tempest*) (Act 2, Scene 2)
Aaron (*Titus Andronicus*)
Malvolio (*Twelfth Night*)
Orsino (*Twelfth Night*)
Launce (*The Two Gentlemen of Verona*)

I have cited specific scenes / speeches against a character, where there is material elsewhere for that character which is not too often used.
This list is by no means exhaustive – other auditioners will have other characters and speeches they've seen too often.

Shakespeare – The Actors' Writer

Shakespeare, and others, wrote for a theatre that had minimal sets and an audience that did not sit quietly watching – they reacted like a modern football crowd. (Conditions that they are attempting to recreate at *Shakespeare's Globe* theatre on London's South Bank.) He had no lighting beyond available daylight and the occasional flare or candle, no sophisticated special effects and no modern sound systems. There was some live music and the occasional drum, trumpet, cornet, and so on, but all the emphasis was on the power of the excitingly spoken word. And that's what Shakespeare gave actors: a brilliant vehicle, his words, that can really help the auditioning actor – also without sets, lighting, and so on. He also had incredible insights into how people 'tick', in a way that wasn't really generally understood until about a hundred years ago – famously through Freud and in the acting world through Stanislavski. Of course other writers of his period, and after, also 'dug inside how people work', but not so much for the theatre. There is a story about a man after seeing his first Shakespeare production: 'Hey, this guy knew about Freud three-hundred years before Freud.'

Shakespeare the Man

We have a number of tantalising facts about the real person, but not enough to write a definitive biography. One thing we are sure of is that he managed to make a good living out of writing and staging plays – he had a commercial eye for what would attract audiences. He looked for popular subjects and tried to avoid controversy by writing plays set either remote in time and / or set in other countries. (Only *The Merry Wives of Windsor* is set overtly in the Elizabethan here-and-now, and that doesn't contain any kings, princes and so on – people who if offended could be highly dangerous.) He didn't write contemporary satires to attract audiences – unlike Ben Jonson, his friend and nearest rival as a playwright – and he seems to have avoided any trouble with the authorities, unlike Jonson who spent time in prison. I think that because he didn't have any political axe to grind, he concentrated on the people in his plays rather than contemporary politics. Issues relevant to an Elizabethan are largely only of interest to an historian of subsequent generations. I believe Shakespeare's apolitical approach and his concentration on the personalities involved helped to ensure his immortality. I'm not saying that he didn't write about politics at all, his plays are full of examples; but he didn't take sides. For example, though there is a lot in *The Merchant of Venice* which is anti-Semitic (shockingly so to a modern audience), Shylock, the money-lender, has some wonderfully sympathetic moments including this (from Act 3, Scene 1): 'I am a Jew. Hath not a Jew eyes? Hath not a Jew hands, organs, dimensions, senses, affections, passions? Fed with the same food, hurt with the same weapons, subject to the same diseases, healed by the same means, warmed and cooled by the same winter and summer as a Christian is? If you prick us, do we not bleed? If you tickle us, do we not laugh? If you poison us, do we not die? And if you wrong us, shall we not revenge?'

As a playwright Shakespeare wasn't working in isolation, he was a member of several acting companies, principally the *Chamberlain's Men* (later known as the *King's Men*). I'd like to suggest that *The Complete Works* came not just from one man but through the energy and ideas generated by groups of people working closely together. A man called 'Shakespeare' may have written a lot of the words, but he must have used their experiences to inspire much of the detail. And, knowing actors, I'm sure they had plenty of their own suggestions – good and bad – that were incorporated into the scripts we now have. This is the cradle, the sustenance and encouragement that nurtured the 'genius' we label 'Shakespeare'. Over half a century later another genius, Sir Isaac Newton, the scientist, wrote, 'If I have seen further it is by standing on the shoulders of giants.' I suggest the same could be said of Shakespeare and his plays.

Elizabethan England

Not only was he almost certainly helped by his actors, but also by the comparatively stable political climate of the first Elizabethan age. As often happens in his history plays, the threat of invasion (and vice-versa) was common in the reigns of Queen Elizabeth I's predecessors. This required armies and ships, which were a huge drain on the national exchequer and when she ascended the throne England was not very well off. Her immediate predecessor (and elder sister), Mary, was a Catholic; Elizabeth, a Protestant, was a ripe target for Catholic France and Spain – England's principal rivals. There were also a number of people in England who thought that Protestantism had gone too far and would have welcomed an invasion. However, the two continental countries were at loggerheads and ignored

England until the Spanish Armada in 1588, thirty years after Elizabeth had ascended the throne. In the interim the English ships had been used for lucrative trade and exploration, thus building a strong economy, strong enough to fund the soldiers and sailors for the defeat of the potential invaders by the time of the Armada; and strong enough to support the social welfare of the nation. 'We were just in a financial position to afford Shakespeare at the moment when he presented himself.' (J. M. Keynes, Economist)

Elizabethan English

Elizabeth was the most extraordinary woman, highly intelligent and literate, and she used her power for the sake of the people, not just for her own ends, as most previous monarchs had done. She created a nation, with the help of some brilliant chief ministers, which had 'a zest and an energy and a love of life that had hardly been known before' (Anthony Burgess). This 'feel-good' factor, that modern politicians yearn for, created a new pride in the English language. Previously, Latin had held sway through the church, over the bulk of printed literature and throughout the limited education provision that existed then. People spoke to each other in various English dialects, but the use of the language in written form was extremely limited. Anything important was written in Latin, with its very strict rules of grammar and spelling – but there were virtually no official rules of spelling and grammar for English. Witness, the varying spellings that we have of Shakespeare's own name: 'Shaxpere', 'Shogspar', 'Choxper', and so on. These arise because each writer of the name (or any word) would write down the sound of what he'd heard as he would like to spell it. The written English of that time was 'not fixed and elegant and controlled by academics' (Anthony Burgess) – it was a language ripe for exploration and development, as the sailors were doing with material goods in the new world.

All this lack of regulation means that it is very common for Shakespeare's characters to commit what we would now consider to be grammatical howlers, for instance plural subjects combined with singular verbs and seemingly non-sensical changes in tense. However, he was writing down (in elevated form) how people speak and these 'howlers' often reflect the characters' state of mind.

The Plots of Shakespeare's Plays

The commercial playwright had to write plays that he could be reasonably sure would attract an audience and took his plots from existing sources that would be generally known and appeal to a paying public. Early works included *The Comedy of Errors,* a free adaptation of a well known Roman comedy of confused identity and *Titus Andronicus*, a sex and sadism horror that would put today's film censors into a complete spin. The three parts of *Henry VI* and *Richard III* are based on historical accounts of one of England's most troubled times which were finally resolved by the acquisition of the throne by Henry VII, grandfather of the ever-popular Queen Elizabeth I – an event which happens at the end of *Richard III*. A modern equivalent might be dramatically to chart Winston Churchill's life from his 'wilderness years' (forced out of politics) to the triumph of the surrender of Nazi Germany.

Another aspect of this commercialism was the 'megabucks' that could be made by special one-off performances for rich patrons. For example, *Macbeth* was probably written for performance before King James I (Elizabeth I's successor). Banquo, one of Macbeth's victims in the play, was reputedly an ancestor of James; Shakespeare radically altered the available historical record to ensure that the King was not offended and included references to witchcraft, breast-feeding and tobacco – subjects very close to James' heart.

Some Significant Speeches in Shakespeare's Plays

It's not just the plots that Shakespeare adapted from known sources, he even adapted other people's words. For example in the court scene of *Henry VIII* (Act 2, Scene 4), Queen Katherine's wonderful speech beginning 'Sir, I desire you do me right and justice...' is an almost direct copy of what she actually said, according to the historical record. Enobarbus' famous speech 'The barge she sat in...' in *Antony and Cleopatra* (Act 2, Scene 2) is very close to a translation from Plutarch's *Life of Antonius*.

Shakespeare's Texts

Four hundred years on, it is difficult to be sure that every word in a Shakespeare play is exactly as he first wrote it. The problems with his play-texts begin with the fact that then there was no such thing as a law of copyright. That wasn't to arrive for another hundred years. Once a play was in print, anyone could simply copy and sell their own version with no royalties going to the original writer. Worse than this, once in print, other companies could put on their own productions in competition. So Shakespeare himself had very few of his own plays printed. About five years after Shakespeare's death, two of his actors John Heminge and Henry Condell put together what scripts they had into print: *The First Folio*, the first – nearly – *Complete Works*.

Amongst their sources were:

(a) Some of the original hand-written cue-scripts (just the individual actor's lines and his cue lines).
(b) Some previously published editions of individual plays, the 'Quarto' editions. ('Quarto' literally means the size of a piece of paper created by folding a whole sheet twice so as to form four leaves or eight pages. 'Folio' means folding that sheet once to make two leaves or four pages.)
(c) The memories of surviving actors.

None of these can be sworn to being entirely accurate because:

(a) Even the best handwriting of the time is sometimes hard to decipher. (We don't have any texts in Shakespeare's own hand.)
(b) Printing in his time wasn't entirely accurate. Think of having to place every letter, space and punctuation mark – each in the form of an individually-moulded piece of lead – into a frame that then went onto the presses. *The Complete Works* (with *The Two Noble Kinsmen*, which is not always included) total about 950,000 words, which is over five million characters; i.e. an average of roughly 25,000 words and 137,000 characters per play. Also some of the Quarto editions were printed from manuscripts written down during performances by people trying to 'pirate' the plays (often known as 'Bad Quartos').
(c) Sometimes actors have very accurate memories for lines they've said on stage; sometimes they improve on what the playwright actually wrote down; and sometimes, the lesser ones make a hash of the playwright's intentions.

Shakespeare probably didn't write every word anyway. There are at least four other writers who almost certainly contributed to what we now know as *The Complete Works*. It also seems to me likely given the circumstances in which Shakespeare wrote – for a specific company of actors – that they might well each have had their individual 'say' in the details of what their characters said and some of their ideas incorporated.

Further confusion is added by the fact that just one copy of a Quarto or Folio edition would be printed, proof-read and corrected, then a second copy would be printed, proof-read and corrected, and so on. Nobody knows whether these time-consuming processes were undertaken for every individual copy, but (to date) nobody has yet found two identical copies of *The First Folio* from the roughly 230 that survive.

There has been such a mass of intellectual detective work trying to establish a perfect version of the text that I believe it is easy to get the impression of a super-human being whose works must be approached with over-weening reverence. Shakespeare was a human being like the rest of us. He was possessed of a brilliant feel for the use of language and how people really feel deep down inside.

I do not say all this to try to bring Shakespeare down from his pedestal; I say it to humanise a man whom others have deified. I don't deny that a nation needs her heroes, but I think that England has elevated 'The Bard' overmuch. True he was part of an innovative (even revolutionary) group that has rarely been matched for its degree of positive development. But, in order to bring life back to his works, nearly four centuries after his death, we have to feel for him – as a jobbing craftsman needing to sell his wares to make a living. We need to make his creations have real life, rather than being some too often regurgitated ceremony that sounds stale.

Finally, I have to add that without the presiding genius and humanity of Elizabeth I we almost certainly wouldn't have known anything of him at all. Periods of great art arise when the prevailing governments are prepared to invest in their nation's culture.

The Lives and Times of Shakespeare's People

It is obvious to say that life was very different for people in Shakespeare's time. To recreate his characters it is important to have some insight into how 'different'.

Birth and Death

It was quite normal for a baby and / or the mother to die at or soon after birth. It is really only since the second world war that such deaths have become rare in Western society. Even if the child survived the crucial early period, many only managed it to their teens. A working class family would aim to breed as many children as possible as workers to help the family's meagre fortunes. Many women, even if they survived the multiple births, were dead of exhaustion by their thirties. The men had the hazard of the frequent wars. Medicine was very rudimentary – if not grotesquely inaccurate – and too expensive for all but the aristocracy, so disease and malnutrition meant that people, on average, lived about forty years. You were considered grown up by about the age of fourteen and old by your mid-thirties.

The aristocracy were better fed and had access to what medicine was available, but their chances in childbirth weren't much better and overall life-expectancy wasn't that much greater. (Though, the real Richard III's mother managed to live until she was eighty.)

Contraception was available (in fact the first evidence of its use dates back nearly four thousand years), but was generally only used for illicit sex. (A pig's bladder for the men and half a lemon for the women, for instance.)

Marriage

In Elizabethan England the age of consent was twelve and it was common for women to give birth in their early teens. Lady Capulet says to her fourteen year old daughter Juliet:

> Well, think of marriage now. Younger than you
> Here in Verona, ladies of esteem,
> Are made already mothers. By my count
> I was your mother much upon these years
> That you are now a maid. (*Romeo and Juliet*, Act 1, Scene 3)

Prior to this period dynastic marriages often took place at even younger ages – for example, the real Richard II's wife, Isabel, was seven when she married him. This occurred when important families wanted to expand their power and possessions by alliance through marriage – equivalent to modern corporate mergers. The marriage partners often had no say in the course of events designed for them.

Democracy

Although the idea of running England through a democratic system started to evolve some three hundred years before Shakespeare, the monarch was still very much in charge – if he or she was strong and ruthless enough. Parliament consisted of the nobility, senior churchmen and representatives of the general population. However, it wasn't a democracy as we would now think of it; more a collection of power groupings who used military muscle to get their way. The nobility had the threat of their private armies; the church (prior to Henry VIII's break with the Roman Catholic church) could threaten to call on military aid from fellow catholic countries. There were also representatives from each town big enough and two knights from each shire (or county) – but these people couldn't call on armies to back up a point, so they had very little actual influence on major issues. Right up to the latter half of the nineteenth century only a small proportion of the male population of the 'civilised' world was allowed to vote; a certain level of wealth and / or literacy being the usual qualification. In Great Britain women had to wait for the twentieth century to be allowed to vote.

Law and Order

There was no national police force and the legal system was fairly arbitrary – generally, favouring the rich. It was comparatively easy to commit and cover up crimes, if you were clever about it. It was also fairly easy to be arrested for something you hadn't done if you were vulnerable and someone with the necessary finances wanted you imprisoned.

Travel and Communications

The only forms of land travel were either on foot or using a four-footed animal, the horse being much the fastest. The latter were too expensive for the ordinary man and consequently the majority of ordinary people would never leave their home town or village. Even those who became soldiers would travel by foot. All this meant that transmitting messages and moving armies took an inordinate amount of time.

Even someone with exceptionally fast horses could only travel at an average of about twenty miles an hour, so it would take at least a day to travel from London to York, for instance. If you did ride this far, only stopping to change to fresh horses, you'd be utterly wrecked by the time you got there.

Taxation

In medieval times the monarch really only needed taxes to pay for wars, his general living expenses came from income from property he owned. By Shakespeare's time the tax system was more extensive in order also to pay for the ever expanding machinery of government. The ruling powers would, arbitrarily, invent a tax to cover an immediate financial problem. The concept of 'fairness' in taxation doesn't really occur until the late eighteenth century and 'income tax' was first introduced in 1799.

The Church

The church had enormous influence on people's lives, the power of the concept of 'God' was all prevailing – with no alternative view on the way the world worked. All but the most widely read would not challenge the idea that in order to have a good 'after life', you'd have to conform to the church's dictates in this life. Science was only just beginning to question some of the church's teachings – coincidentally, a prime-mover of this questioning, Galileo Galilei, was born in the same year as Shakespeare (1564), though it wasn't until the year of Shakespeare's death (1616) that he was taken to task by the church authorities for his revolutionary ideas.

It is also worth mentioning that the other most wonderful publication during the reign of King James I was the English language version of the Bible, which was still in common use until very recently.

Education

Education was just beginning to expand. It wasn't just the wealthy who could learn to read and write. Free schools were opening up, paid for by more enlightened boroughs and open to children of worthy local citizens, i.e. the elite of the middle-classes. The lessons consisted mostly of Latin studies, the language in which most of the limited printed matter of that time was issued; and a drilling in of their duties toward God, the sovereign and 'all others in their degree'. The poor had to wait until the late nineteenth century for the right to universal education.

Sanitation

Even in London there was no such thing as main drainage systems; sewage was simply dumped in the street – to be carried away by the rains, when they happened. Plague was a regular occurrence and public places such as theatres were closed when it struck to prevent further infection. Country areas, like Shakespeare's Stratford, smelt sweeter and people's health was generally better than in cramped and stinking London.

Light and Heat

Burning what you could acquire was the only source of these basics; there were no national fuel grids of any kind.

Primitive but survivable, England was just moving from an aristo-cratically run society to one where even the lowliest individual was beginning to matter – only thirty-three years after Shakespeare died, the English executed their king and parliament ruled without an absolute monarch for eleven years.

Within the confines of this book I can only briefly evoke a few basic aspects of life in Shakespeare's time. A character's life is not just battles and loves, won and lost; it is also the ordinary, everyday aspects that the dramatist misses out because they are not dramatic and don't serve the life of the play. In order to bring those characters to life you should find out as much as you can about how their lives were lived outside the action of the play.

Auditioning Shakespeare

Shakespeare acting – at root – is not different from 'modern' acting. Where it is different is in that his language uses words, phrases and expressions we no longer use; and (more importantly) the circumstances are invariably far away from our direct experience. It is your job (whether aspiring or professional) to steep yourself in the culture that influenced his plays if you are to perform pieces from them.

Many actors argue that doing an audition speech is a desperately artificial way of having their worth assessed. I would tend to agree but, however much you may hate them, you will periodically have to do them. Of course it's an artificial situation, but isn't acting about making artifice seem real? There are ways of making them work – think of Bob Hoskins in *Who Framed Roger Rabbit* and Steve Martin in *Dead Men Don't Wear Plaid*, both acting with beings who weren't really there.

I have 'road-tested' all the speeches contained in this book; it is now your job to research and rehearse those of your choice. You also need to prepare yourself for the varying circumstances you could be asked to perform them in. Think of an audition speech as a 'mini-play'; you are going to present a 'mini-production' of it.

Preparations

There are a number of things to consider before you start rehearsing your speeches:

Iambic Pentameters

Apart from the unfamiliar words, phrases and expressions, this verse form (popular in Shakespeare's time) is off-putting – on the page – to many people. I think it's a good idea to think of it not as poetry, but as verbal music: that is words and phraseology that people use when they have a real need to express themselves or 'touch the souls of others'. A good playwright not only writes good stories and creates credible characters, but also writes in language that will 'grab' an audience – language that has a music of its own. Shakespeare was a master of verbal music, along with Samuel Beckett, Harold Pinter, Sam Shepard, Edward Albee, David Mamet, Arthur Miller, Alan Ayckbourn, and too many more to mention. It is not so much plots that make great playwrights, it is their use of language.

Rhymes

Some of the verse rhymes, which can sound terribly forced and unnatural if you emphasise the rhyming words too much. You can't avoid the rhyme, but it's important to make it sound natural and not forced (as poetry is often read).

-èd

All the accent on the 'e' means is that you pronounce the 'ed' where you normally wouldn't. For example: we'd normally pronounce 'imagined' not sounding the 'e'; but if it's written 'imaginèd', you pronounce it 'imagin-ed'. Some editions (mostly older ones) miss out the 'e' if it is not to be pronounced and insert an apostrophe instead and leave it there, unaccented, if it should be sounded.

i', th', and so on

Some people balk at these foreshortened words. All this means is that you pronounce them literally as written. Listen to yourself and others in normal conversation to observe how many letters we miss out.

Making Sense

As you start out on a speech look at the sense, ignore the verse. Look for the full stops, even if they arrive halfway through a line. Then, look at each clause within that sentence; then put that whole sentence together to make the sense of the whole of it. Then, start to put the sense of the whole speech together – still ignoring the verse.

Finally, look at what words begin and end a line of verse, they may have a significance that you haven't previously recognised. After you've been through all the processes of finding and becoming the character, the positioning of these words may add to your understanding of him.

'The multitudinous seas incarnadine' (*Macbeth*, Act 2, Scene 2)

In his musical on the life of William Blake, *Tyger*, Adrian Mitchell had Shakespeare appear as a cowboy, or 'pen-slinger': 'I can drop 'em with one line'. It's that turn of phrase (that has now degraded into the 'sound-bite') that makes Shakespeare's language so exciting. It is your job also to make it 'real' for the character – don't sing it, believe it.

Preconceptions

With the famous characters, forget any preconceived notions you may have, e.g. Hamlet is 'mad', Juliet is 'wet', and so on. Part of Shakespeare's insight is that he created (mostly) very real people who may primarily exhibit one aspect of human behaviour through the circumstances of the play; but, as in life, there's far more to them than that. Think how often you meet someone new, get the chance to get to know them and find that there's 'far more than meets the eye'. The aim of this book is to steer people away from these too well-known characters, but the same kind of preconception can take over and dominate the performance. For instance, Iachimo (from *Cymbeline*) seems like a classic 'baddie', but in his eyes he simply wants to win his bet – and he does have moments of conscientious scruple.

Selecting Speeches

Read through the speeches in this book and see which ones create sparks for you, without necessarily fully understanding the content. (Largely, ignore the notes and character description at first, these come later.) If the 'music' of the words feels good then you are over halfway towards finding a speech suitable for you. It can also be a good idea to read them – carefully – out loud, without any sense of 'acting' them. Then read the 'Character Descriptions' to see if the characters are appropriate to you (age, type, and so on) and assess whether it's worth going further.

Don't be tempted simply to go for ones with the most spectacular emotions – auditioners want to see real feelings not flashy melodrama.

Length

An audition speech doesn't need to be more than about two minutes long and can be shorter, which can feel too short whilst you are doing it. Interestingly, Shakespeare speeches often work better when they're even shorter; I think that it may be something to do with the fact that he packs so much into his characters – a few of his words can speak such volumes. Many people think that they're not doing enough with fourteen or fifteen lines of verse – which will probably last only about one and a half minutes. Providing the speech has a complete journey to it, it doesn't matter if it's this short. On the other hand, you can lose your audience if you go on for forty lines. You may argue that there is no way you can show enough of your skills as an actor in such a short time. True, you can't show everything, but you can give a very good indication of your potential – like a good television commercial.

How Many?

For too many people the 'Shakespeare' is the speech they least want to do, and they strain even to get the minimum (of one) together. I think this is very silly. The best results I've seen have come from people who've worked on four or five – and even more. Especially if you are new to acting in his language (as opposed to just reading it), working on several speeches at once can give you a much broader insight into his world. And if you begin to fall out of love with one or two of them, you've got the others to fall back on. If you only start with one, you've got to start all over again if you become dissatisfied with it.

Verse or Prose

Some auditioners insist that you present verse speeches, so it is important to have at least one in your repertoire.

Read the Whole Play

Next, read the whole play (slowly and carefully), read a few commentaries and if possible talk about the play and its people with someone who knows it. It can be helpful to read a summary first and then read the play, but bear in mind that these merely sum up the major plot and what happens to the people, without giving much psychological insight.

When a play is completely new to me, I find it helpful to copy out the cast list and write notes about each character as they appear. Obviously this takes time, but it's extremely helpful to the process of getting under the skins of the characters.

On the other hand, don't spend hours flicking backwards and forwards to the footnotes to try to understand every line. A general sense of the people and events is all that's needed at this stage (and how your character fits in). It's important to get some idea of the flow of the whole thing – too much stopping and starting can make you lose any idea of the whole.

It is not sufficient just to read the scene a chosen speech is from – you won't gain proper insight into where your character is coming from.

The Immediate Context

When you've got hold of who your 'person' is, build up the stimuli that affect him: the other people (present and / or influential), the circumstances (place, time, and so on) – as well as the immediate provocation for the speech.

The Details

One of the fundamental keys to good acting is the degree of detail with which you imagine the above. For example, if your character is in a castle, it's not any old castle, it's somebody's home – maybe your character's own. Look at pictures and, if possible, visit castles that are preserved as they were lived in (ruins will only give a partial impression). Try to absorb the details of what it might have been like to live in one. (Touch bare stone walls, that'll give you a very strong feel for medieval living.) In short, find out (and imagine if you can't find out) as much as you can about the 'ordinary' bits of the life your character might have led that are not mentioned in the play.

The Clothes

A supremely important 'detail' is the clothes your character(s) would wear. I'm not suggesting that you dress in period clothes, but to imagine the feel of wearing them, or whatever is appropriate to the period and circumstances of the speech. One of the principal omissions I see is the sense of wearing a weapon, which is common to many characters. Different clothes, including shoes, make you move in different ways.

The Notes

Begin to understand the details of the words and phrases of the speech through using my notes and those from a good edition of the complete play. (See my Bibliography at the end of this book for suggestions on this.) Write out your own translation into modern English if you find that useful, but don't become wedded to that translation, you'll find it hard to go back to the original. It's probably best to write it out and then throw it away, so you get a better idea of the sense without becoming fixed on specific modern words and phrases.

The notes attached to some established editions can confuse with cross-references irrelevant to acting. They may be written 'about' the character, rather than for the person acting him. On the other hand, the notes in some exam text 'note' books can tend to over-simplify.

Research

When there are real people involved it can be useful to research what we know about them. However, Shakespeare had a rather 'tabloid' attitude to the truth. The 'history plays' are based on real historical events (*Henry VIII* ends only thirty one years before Shakespeare's birth), but, like many other playwrights since, he doesn't always follow historical facts as we now understand them. Sometimes this is because the then limited historical research was inaccurate; sometimes it is because reality doesn't necessarily make good drama (this is common to all drama); sometimes (especially in *Henry VIII*) he couldn't risk the wrath of current sensibilities; and possibly sometimes he was writing too fast to research properly or he was simply lazy. Do research, but don't let inaccuracies confuse you: take what you can from history but the information gleaned from the play must finally be the deciding factor.

Learning the Lines

Don't sit down and learn the lines parrot fashion. In all this research into the background detail, keep going back to the play, your character and his speech, to check that what you've found out (and used your imagination to create) still fits with what's in the text. You will find those lines simply start 'going in' the more you understand them and the circumstances of them being spoken.

If you find that parts will not 'go in' by this process of study and absorption, then it is almost certain that you haven't fully understood what they mean.

Don't Generalise!

Because it's a speech too may people tend to generalise, and it all comes out sounding the same. In life very few people anticipate speaking at such length except in specific circumstances. You should think of it as a series of connected thoughts and ideas – the circumstances stimulate the first thought to come out as words, then another arrives and needs to be spoken, and another, and so on. Usually, at the beginning, you should convey the impression you don't know what you are going to say at the end.

Soliloquies

Shakespeare is famous for these and some people think that they should always be addressed to the audience. With obvious exceptions (the Chorus and some of the clowns, for instance), I believe they are the characters talking to themselves – 'for' the audience. When we talk to ourselves in life we keep it private and mutter. In acting we have to communicate to an audience – this is one of the fundamental differences between the 'being' process above and acting. You've got to go through the first stage of 'being' before you can go on to 'act' your speech. Don't try to prepare the other way round.

It's useful to think of soliloquies as the character thinking aloud in order to try to organise his jumbled thoughts.

Difficult to Say Words and Phrases

If you find yourself consistently tripping over a word or phrase, try saying it in isolation – with a lot of over-articulation. Do this slowly and carefully lots of times and you'll find it'll become second nature to you.

Obscure Words and Phrases

I am still amazed by the fact that if the actor understands these – in his soul – the general sense will communicate to whatever audience is watching, and they don't need extra demonstration. This 'understanding' is not simply a mental process, it is a feeling for what the word or phrase means so that it becomes a totally natural thing to say in the circumstances.

First Steps

When you think that you know and understand what your character (or 'person') is talking about and understand their circumstances, start saying the lines out loud – aiming to talk to whomsoever is or are the recipients of the words. Don't think of it as acting; you are slowly beginning to become the 'person' who is saying those words – through the speaking of them combined with all your thinking and research. Take a line or two at a time, and go back over each small section several times until you begin to feel you are emotionally connecting. You should begin to see the circumstances really happening in your imagination. One (pre-drama school) student I taught was really getting inside a Richard II speech; suddenly he stopped and said, 'I can see those f****** horses!' I shouted, 'Keep going!', and when he finished we talked about his experience. The steady research and thought he had put in (over about two months) had paid off. After that he 'saw' those horses regularly when doing this speech, but it wasn't as shocking as the first time – just a normal part of 'being' Richard II. (Incidentally, he had no idea of where this king fitted into English history when he started.)

When you are 'connecting' with your first line or two go on to the next, but use the first as a run up, and steadily on through the speech. (Please note that I still haven't suggested 'learning' the lines yet.)

I'm convinced that creating a character is very similar to the growing process from cradle to maturity.

Rehearsing Your Speeches

After you've done all this preparation you can start rehearsing your speeches, actually becoming the person saying those words in those particular circumstances. If you've prepared thoroughly, you'll be wonderfully surprised at how real, alive and exciting you can now make someone who was created four centuries ago.

Shakespeare's Advice

Hamlet says the following to a group of strolling players:

Speak the speech, I pray you, as I pronounced it to you – trippingly on the tongue; but if you mouth it, as many of your players do, I had as lief the town-crier had spoke my lines. Nor do not saw the air too much with your hand, thus, but use all gently; for in the very torrent, tempest, and as I may say the whirlwind of your passion, you must acquire and beget a temperance that may give it smoothness. O, it offends me to the soul to hear a robustious, periwig-pated fellow tear a passion to tatters, to very rags, to split the ears of the groundlings, who for the most part are capable of nothing but inexplicable dumb shows and noise ...

... Be not too tame, neither; but let your own discretion be your tutor. Suit the action to the word, the word to the action, with this special observance: that you o'erstep not the modesty of nature. For anything so overdone is from the purpose of playing, whose end, both at the first and now, was and is to hold as 'twere the mirror up to nature, to show virtue her own feature, scorn her own image, and the very age and body of the time his form and pressure. Now this over-done, or come tardy off, though it make the unskilful laugh, cannot but make the judicious grieve ...   (*Hamlet*, Act 2, Scene 3)

This is some of the most succinct acting advice ever given – three hundred years before Stanislavski (and others) were completely rethinking how we do acting.

The Speeches

All's Well that Ends Well

Parolles

Parolles is a follower of Bertram, the son of the Countess of Rossillion. He is variously described as a 'coward', a 'blusterer' and a 'very tainted fellow, and full of wickedness'. However, after his exposure as a charlatan later in the play, he shows a strong pragmatism; his self-promoted career as a noble soldier is finished, but he makes the most of his new situation and resolves to become a jester ('There's place and means for every man alive'). He is here talking with Helena, an orphan adopted by the Countess, and secretly in love with Bertram. Parolles arrives and asks her point-blank, 'Are you meditating on virginity?'; she asks him how she might defend hers: 'Unfold to us some warlike resistance'. This is his advice.

Although we are given many guidelines to his character, his age is not really indicated.

I have cut a few lines of Helena's to construct this speech.

---

1   *setting down before* laying siege to
1–2   *blow you up* make you pregnant (literally, explode semen into)
2–3   *be blown up* reach orgasm
3   *Marry* Why, to be sure (a mild swear-word literally meaning, 'by the Virgin Mary')
4   *city* virginity
6   *rational increase* (1) sensible benefit, (2) leads to the increase of ('rational') human beings
      virgin got child conceived
7   *That* That which
      mettle temperament (This is 'metal' in some editions.)
10   *in 't* for it
13   *virginity murders itself* for virginity prevents future children ('virgins')
14   *sanctified limit* consecrated ground
16   *to the very paring* to the last sliver
17   *feeding his own stomach* living ('feeding') on its own pride (at maintaining virginity)
19   *inhibited sin in the canon* prohibited sin in the Scriptures
19–20 *Keep it not; you cannot choose but lose by 't. Out with 't!* Don't hoard your capital (or 'principal'); for you can only lose it. Invest it to earn interest! (He is punning on keeping the 'principle' of 'virginity' or earning interest, by investing in children – this continues to the end of the speech.)
20   *t' one* (This is 'ten' or 'the' in other editions.)

Act 1, Scene 1
Parolles –

1   Man, setting down before you, will undermine and blow you
     up. Virginity being blown down, man will quicklier be blown
     up. Marry, in blowing him down again, with the breach
     yourselves made, you lose your city. It is not politic in the
5   commonwealth of nature to preserve virginity. Loss of
     virginity is rational increase, and there was never virgin got
     till virginity was first lost. That you were made of is mettle to
     make virgins. Virginity, by being once lost, may be ten times
     found; by being ever kept, it is ever lost. 'Tis too cold a
10   companion; away with 't! There's little can be said in 't; 'tis
     against the rule of nature. To speak on the part of virginity is
     to accuse your mothers, which is most infallible disobedience.
     He that hangs himself is a virgin: virginity murders itself, and
     should be buried in highways out of all sanctified limit, as a
15   desperate offendress against nature. Virginity breeds mites,
     much like a cheese; consumes itself to the very paring, and so
     dies with feeding his own stomach. Besides, virginity is
     peevish, proud, idle, made of self-love – which is the most
     inhibited sin in the canon. Keep it not; you cannot choose but
20   lose by 't. Out with 't! Within t' one year it will make itself
     two, which is a goodly increase; and the principal itself not
22   much the worse. Away with 't.

Antony and Cleopatra

Octavius Caesar

Octavius Caesar (Octavian) (63 B.C.–A.D. 14) was the adopted son of Julius Caesar – in fact he was the grandson of Julius' sister. Octavius was a 19-year-old student in Athens when Caesar was assassinated; he immediately asserted himself politically and was soon at the head of an army of pro-Caesar forces – with Antony and Lepidus – that eventually defeated the assassins. The three victors formed the 'Triumvirate' to rule the Roman Empire. Within a few years Antony had started his affair with Cleopatra, queen of Egypt (a Roman conquest), and reports started to reach Octavius that Antony had been neglecting his duties. At this point Octavius is about twenty-three and is talking with Lepidus, very much the weakest of the triumvirs. A messenger has just brought news that a rebel force led by Pompey is massing against the triumvirate. He appeals to the absent Antony.

Antony was very much the mastermind of their military successes and was nearly twenty years older than Octavius.

Octavius became the first emperor of Rome, with the name Augustus, in 27 B.C.

---

2   *bed of Ptolemy* Cleopatra's bed ('Ptolemy' was her dynastic name)
3   *a mirth* mere entertainment
4   *keep the turn of* take turns in
    tippling (persistently) drinking toasts (in hard liquor)
    slave (i.e. Cleopatra, who was queen of a conquered nation)
5   *reel* stagger (drunk)
    stand the buffet endure the punches
6   *knaves that smells of sweat* common ('sweaty') people
7   *As* Although
    composure character
9   *foils* (disgraceful) behaviours
10 *So great a weight in his lightness* All the problems (of ruling the known world) as a result of his irresponsibility
11 *vacancy* (vacuous) leisure
12 *Full surfeits* Stomach disorders
    dryness of his bones syphilis (which was thought to cause a 'dryness of the bones')
13 *Call on him for 't* Call him to account
    confound waste
14 *drums* orders (as in a military drum)
    speaks as loud is as bad
15 *his own state and ours* his and our (public) positions
    chid reprimanded
16 *rate* rebuke
18 *to* against

Act 1, Scene 4
Caesar –

1   You are too indulgent. Let's grant it is not
        Amiss to tumble on the bed of Ptolemy,
        To give a kingdom for a mirth, to sit
        And keep the turn of tippling with a slave,
5   To reel the streets at noon, and stand the buffet
        With knaves that smells of sweat. Say this becomes him –
        As his composure must be rare indeed
        Whom these things cannot blemish – yet must Antony
        No way excuse his foils when we do bear
10   So great weight in his lightness. If he filled
        His vacancy with his voluptuousness,
        Full surfeits and the dryness of his bones
        Call on him for 't. But to confound such time
        That drums him from his sport, and speaks as loud
15   As his own state and ours – 'tis to be chid
        As we rate boys who, being mature in knowledge,
        Pawn their experience to their present pleasure,
18   And so rebel to judgement.

Antony and Cleopatra

Octavius Caesar

Octavius Caesar (Octavian) (63 B.C.–A.D. 14) was the adopted son of
Julius Caesar – in fact he was the grandson of Julius' sister. Octavius was
a 19-year-old student in Athens when Caesar was assassinated; he
immediately asserted himself politically and was soon at the head of an
army of pro-Caesar forces – with Antony and Lepidus – that eventually
defeated the assassins. The three victors formed the 'Triumvirate' to rule
the Roman Empire. Within a few years Antony had started his affair
with Cleopatra, queen of Egypt (a Roman conquest), and reports started
to reach Octavius that Antony had been neglecting his duties. At this
point Octavius is about twenty-three and is talking with Lepidus, very
much the weakest of the triumvirs.

Antony was very much the mastermind of their military successes
and was nearly twenty years older than Octavius.

Octavius became the first emperor of Rome, with the name Augustus,
in 27 B.C.

I have cut Lepidus' short line in the middle of line 17.

---

2   *lascivious wassails* drunken revelling

2–17 (The war he talks about here is the war of Mutina (Modena), 43 B.C., in which Antony was
      defeated by the army of the Roman Senate.)

5   *whom* (i.e. 'famine')

8   *stale* urine

    gilded with a glittering scum on the surface

9   *cough at* turn up their noses at

    deign not refuse

10 *rudest* wildest

12 *browsed* ate from

17 *So much as lanked not* Did not even become thinner

19 *i' th' field* (i.e. to the army)

20 *Pompey* (Gnaeus Pompey, who was in rebellion agaist the triumvirate – he was the younger son
      of Pompey the Great, who was in his turn Julius Caesar's arch rival.)

Act 1, Scene 4
Caesar –

1   Antony,
      Leave thy lascivious wassails! When thou once
      Was beaten from Modena, where thou slew'st
      Hirtius and Pansa, consuls, at thy heel
5   Did famine follow, whom thou fought'st against –
      Though daintily brought up – with patience more
      Than savages could suffer. Thou didst drink
      The stale of horses and the gilded puddle
      Which beasts would cough at. Thy palate then did deign
10   The roughest berry on the rudest hedge.
      Yea, like the stag when snow the pasture sheets,
      The barks of trees thou browsed. On the Alps
      It is reported thou didst eat strange flesh,
      Which some did die to look on. And all this –
15   It wounds thine honour that I speak it now –
      Was borne so like a soldier that thy cheek
      So much as lanked not. Let his shames quickly
      Drive him to Rome. 'Tis time we twain
      Did show ourselves i' th' field; and to that end
20   Assemble we immediate council. Pompey
      Thrives in our idleness.

Coriolanus

Caius Martius Coriolanus

Caius Martius (Marcius) Coriolanus was a legendary Roman general. He is an aristocrat and a brilliant soldier, but he has no time for the ordinary people. Here, the citizens of Rome are rioting over the high price of corn; they principally blame Caius Martius ('He's a very dog to the commonalty') in spite of the military service he has done the country. At first Menenius, his friend and respected by the people, manages to stall them for a while but starts to lose ground in his argument. Then Caius Martius appears and asks them bluntly, 'What's the matter, you dissentious rogues?', one replies sarcastically, 'We have ever your good word', which provokes him to this outburst.

Although known for his arrogant pride he does show some sensitive human touches, particularly with his family.

'Coriolanus' was the title conferred upon him after his victory over the Volscians at Corioles (Act 1, Scene 9). He is generally played middle-aged, but I don't see why he can't be as young as late twenties.

———————————

3   *like nor peace nor war* are satisfied with neither peace nor war (because they are frightened in war and rebelliously express dissatisfactions in peace)

4   *proud* arrogant

6   *no surer* no more loyal than

8   *virtue* particular characteristic

9   *To make him worthy whose offence subdues him* To make a hero of someone who is justly punished

10 *And curse that justice did it* Then to curse the justice that did it

11 *Deserves* Earns
    affections inclinations

17 *now* a moment beforehand

18 *your garland* your hero (The Romans decorated their heroes with garlands, where we now use medals.)

19 *several places* different parts

21 *which else* who otherwise (i.e. those in the crowd)

Act 1, Scene 1
Martius –

1   He that will give good words to thee will flatter
       Beneath abhorring. What would you have, you curs
       That like nor peace nor war? The one affrights you,
       The other makes you proud. He that trusts to you,
5   Where he should find you lions, finds you hares;
       Where foxes, geese. You are no surer, no,
       Than is the coal of fire upon the ice,
       Or hailstone in the sun. Your virtue is
       To make him worthy whose offence subdues him,
10   And curse that justice did it. Who deserves greatness
       Deserves your hate; and your affections are
       A sick man's appetite, who desires most that
       Which would increase his evil. He that depends
       Upon your favours swims with fins of lead,
15   And hews down oaks with rushes. Hang ye! Trust ye?
       With every minute you do change a mind
       And call him noble that was now your hate,
       Him vile that was your garland. What's the matter,
       That in these several places of the city
20   You cry against the noble senate, who,
       Under the gods, keep you in awe, which else
22   Would feed on one another?

Cymbeline

Iachimo

Iachimo (or Giacomo or Jachimo) is a young Italian gentleman who meets Posthumus Leonatus, a young British nobleman, in Rome. Posthumus has been banished because he secretly married Imogen, daughter to King Cymbeline of Britain; the King wanted his daughter to marry his stepson, Cloten. Posthumus claims that Imogen is more virtuous than all other women; Iachimo is sceptical and wagers that he can seduce her. He travels to Britain and meets Imogen, claims that Posthumus is leading a dissolute life and encourages her to seek revenge by sleeping with him. She angrily rebuffs him and he pretends that he was merely testing her virtue. She is mollified and agrees to help him by keeping a trunk of his valuables in the safest possible place – her own bedchamber. Imogen is not long asleep.

Although the above may seem to make him seem somewhat callous, he does have moments of decency, e.g. when he first meets Imogen he doesn't think he can go through with it.

I have cut five lines from the original speech (and added a few words to keep the metre) to make this a more manageable length for audition.

----

2   *Cytherea* Venus, the goddess of love
3   *bravely* beautifully
     lily (An emblem of chastity.)
6   *they do 't* (i.e. her lips kiss each other.)
9   *lights* (i.e. her eyes)
14 *arras* wall-hangings
     figures carvings
15 *notes* marks
16 *movables* moveable objects
18 *ape* mimic
     dull heavy
19 *be her sense but as a monument* let her be as insensible as an effigy on a tomb
21 *Gordian knot* (Intricate knot which the Phrygian king Gordius tied and defied anyone to untie.)
25 *cinque* five (pronounced 'sank')
26 *voucher* proof
34 *bare the raven's eye* (Ravens were believed to sleep facing east and waken at sunrise.)

Cymbeline

Act 2, Scene 2
Iachimo –

Imogen sleeps. Iachimo comes from the trunk

1 The crickets sing, and man's o'er-laboured sense
Repairs itself by rest. O Cytherea,
How bravely thou becom'st thy bed! Fresh lily,
And whiter than the sheets! That I might touch!
5 But kiss, one kiss! Rubies unparagoned,
How dearly they do 't! 'Tis her breathing that
Perfumes the chamber thus. The flame o' th' taper
Bows toward her, and would under-peep her lids,
To see th' enclosèd lights, now canopied
10 Under these windows, white and azure, laced
With blue of heaven's own tinct. But my design –
To note the chamber. I will write all down.
Such and such pictures, there the window, such
Th' adornment of her bed, the arras, figures –
15 Ah, but some natural notes about her body,
Above ten thousand meaner movables
Would testify t' enrich mine inventory.
O sleep, thou ape of death, lie dull upon her,
And be her sense but as a monument
20 Thus in a chapel lying. Come off, come off;
As slippery as the Gordian knot was hard.
[*He takes the bracelet from her arm*]
'Tis mine, and this will witness outwardly,
As strongly as the conscience does within,
To th' madding of her lord. On her left breast
25 A mole, cinque-spotted, like the crimson drops
I' th' bottom of a cowslip. Here's a voucher
Stronger than ever law could make. This secret
Will force him think I have picked the lock and ta'en
The treasure of her honour. No more. To what end?
30 Why should I write this down that's riveted,
Screwed to my memory? On now, I have enough.
To th' trunk again, and shut the spring of it.
Swift, swift, you dragons of the night, that dawning
May bare the raven's eye! I lodge in fear,
35 Though this a heavenly angel, hell is here. [*Clock strikes*]
One, two, three. Time, time!   *Exit into the trunk*

Cymbeline

Posthumus Leonatus

Posthumus Leonatus is a 'poor but worthy gentleman' who is in love with Imogen, daughter of King Cymbeline. They marry secretly, but the King is furious (because he wanted her to marry his stepson, Cloten) and banishes Posthumus. Before they part, they swear fidelity and exchange tokens of their love. He goes to Rome where he meets Iachimo, a young Italian gentleman, and boasts of his wife's faithfulness to him. Iachimo is sceptical and wagers all his gold that he can seduce her; Posthumus accepts the bet and Iachimo travels to England on his quest. He has just returned to Rome and presented Posthumus with seemingly irrefutable evidence of success ('Your lady being so easy'). Posthumus has just been left alone.

---

1   *to be* (i.e. born)
2   *half-workers* collaborators (in procreation)
     bastards all (This is 'all bastards' in some editions.)
6   *Dian* Diana (goddess of chastity, and other things)
7   *nonpareil* without equal (in virtue)
11 *pudency* modesty
12 *Saturn* (Roman god and, then, the furthest observable planet from the sun – therefore, the coldest.)
14 *yellow* sallow
15 *at first* (i.e. at first meeting)
16 *full-acorned* boar, a German one (Known for their great strength, ferocity and sexual hunger.)
18 *what he looked for should oppose* what resistance ('opposition') he should expect (from her)
20 *motion* impulse
25 *change of prides* one excess after another
26 *Nice longing* Promiscuity
     mutability changeability
30 *still* constantly
33 *greater skill* wiser
34 *they have their will* (i.e. and therefore destroy themselves)

30

Cymbeline

Act 2, Scene 5 (Scene 4 in some editions)
Posthumus –

Enter Posthumus

1   Is there no way for men to be, but women
    Must be half-workers? We are bastards all,
    And that most venerable man, which I
    Did call my father, was I know not where
5   When I was stamped. Some coiner with his tools
    Made me a counterfeit; yet my mother seemed
    The Dian of that time: so doth my wife
    The nonpareil of this. O vengeance, vengeance!
    Me of my lawful pleasure she restrained,
10   And prayed me oft forbearance; did it with
    A pudency so rosy, the sweet view on 't
    Might well have warmed old Saturn; that I thought her
    As chaste as unsunned snow. O, all the devils!
    This yellow Iachimo in an hour – was 't not? –
15   Or less – at first? Perchance he spoke not, but
    Like a full-acorned boar, a German one,
    Cried 'O!' and mounted; found no opposition
    But what he looked for should oppose and she
    Should from encounter guard. Could I find out
20   The woman's part in me – for there's no motion
    That tends to vice in man, but I affirm
    It is the woman's part; be it lying, note it,
    The woman's; flattering, hers; deceiving, hers;
    Lust and rank thoughts, hers, hers; revenges, hers;
25   Ambitions, covetings, change of prides, disdain,
    Nice longing, slanders, mutability,
    All faults that man can name, nay, that hell knows,
    Why, hers in part or all, but rather all –
    For even to vice
30   They are not constant, but are changing still;
    One vice, but of a minute old, for one
    Not half so old as that. I'll write against them,
    Detest them, curse them; yet 'tis greater skill
    In a true hate to pray they have their will.
35   The very devils cannot plague them better.   *Exit*

Cymbeline

Pisanio

Pisanio is the faithful servant of the 'poor but worthy' Posthumus Leonatus. His master is banished for secretly marrying Imogen, daughter of King Cymbeline; Pisanio remains behind to serve his new mistress. Exiled in Rome, Posthumus is persuaded that his wife is unfaithful and writes to Pisanio telling him to kill her. Pisanio has just received the letter. He is generally perceived as being a similar age to his 'young' master, but I don't see why he couldn't be almost any 'active' age.

It would then have been as bad for a servant to disobey his master as for a soldier to disobey an officer – even if the junior sincerely believed the senior was wrong.

---

2   *Leonatus* (This is the more familiar name for his master.)
7   *truth* fidelity (to you)
    undergoes holds out against
9   *take in* conquer
10 *Thy mind to her* How you think of her ('her' is 'hers' in some editions which, I believe, unnecessarily complicates the line.)
12 *Upon* As a consequence of
15 *How look I* How can you believe
17 *So much as this fact comes to* For this is what it (i.e. what you've asked me to do) amounts to
21 *a fedary* an accomplice (This is spelled 'feodary' in some editions.)
23 *I am ignorant in what I am commanded.* I must pretend I know nothing of these orders.

32

Act 3, Scene 2
Pisanio –

Enter Pisanio, with a letter

1 How? Of adultery? Wherefore write you not
   What monster's her accuser? Leonatus,
   O master, what a strange infection
   Is fall'n into thy ear! What false Italian,
5 As poisonous tongued as handed, hath prevailed
   On thy too ready hearing? Disloyal? No.
   She's punished for her truth; and undergoes,
   More goddess-like than wife-like, such assaults
   As would take in some virtue. O my master,
10 Thy mind to her is now as low as were
   Thy fortunes. How? That I should murder her,
   Upon the love and truth and vows which I
   Have made to thy command? I, her? Her blood?
   If it be so to do good service, never
15 Let me be counted serviceable. How look I,
   That I should seem to lack humanity
   So much as this fact comes to? [*Reads*] 'Do 't. The letter
   That I have sent her, by her own command
   Shall give thee opportunity.' O damned paper,
20 Black as the ink that's on thee! Senseless bauble,
   Art thou a fedary for this act, and look'st
   So virgin-like without? Lo, here she comes.
23 I am ignorant in what I am commanded.

Henry V

The Boy

The Boy is the servant of Bardolph, Pistol and Nym – a ragbag collection of soldiers in Henry V's army in France, and cronies of the late Sir John Falstaff. Although we learn very little else about him, he is obviously educated (unusual at that time) as he later interprets between Pistol and a captive French soldier in Act 4, Scene 4.

King Henry V has just given his famous 'Once more unto the breach' speech to encourage his soldiers at the siege of Harfleur; the reluctant Bardolph, Pistol and Nym are hustled off to the fight by an officer leaving the Boy to reflect alone.

Later, he is left with other boys to guard the English baggage train during the battle of Agincourt – they are all massacred by retreating French soldiers.

1	*swashers* blustering braggarts
2	*boy* servant
	though even if
	should (This is 'would' in some editions.)
3	*man to me* more of a man than I am
	antics buffoons
4	*white-livered* cowardly
5	*'a* he (and at lines 7, 10 and 11)
7	*breaks words* bandies (hostile) words
7–8	*keeps whole weapons* keeps his weapons in one piece (i.e. 'whole' – with the implication that he never uses them in action)
12	*broke any man's head* hit anyone's head so that it bled
13	*anything* (i.e. however useless)
14	*'purchase'* plunder (i.e. the spoils of war)
17	*piece of service* (military) bravery (ironic)
	carry coals (1) put up with insults without retaliating; (2) do the dirtiest work
18	*as familiar with men's pockets* as familiar with pick-pocketing
19	*makes much against* strongly offends
23	*against my weak stomach* against my sensitivities
	cast it up abandon it

Act 3, Scene 2
Boy –

1   As young as I am, I have observed these three swashers. I am
boy to them all three, but all they three, though they should
serve me, could not be man to me; for indeed three such antics
do not amount to a man. For Bardolph, he is white-livered

5   and red-faced – by the means whereof 'a faces it out, but
fights not. For Pistol, he hath a killing tongue and a quiet
sword – by the means whereof 'a breaks words, and keeps
whole weapons. For Nym, he hath heard that men of few
words are the best men, and therefore he scorns to say his

10   prayers, lest 'a should be thought a coward. But his few bad
words are matched with as few good deeds – for 'a never
broke any man's head but his own, and that was against a
post, when he was drunk. They will steal anything, and call it
'purchase'. Bardolph stole a lute-case, bore it twelve leagues,

15   and sold it for three halfpence. Nym and Bardolph are sworn
brothers in filching, and in Calais they stole a fire-shovel; I
knew by that piece of service the men would carry coals. They
would have me as familiar with men's pockets as their gloves
or their handkerchiefs – which makes much against my

20   manhood, if I should take from another's pocket to put into
mine; for it is plain pocketing up of wrongs. I must leave
them, and seek some better service. Their villainy goes

23   against my weak stomach, and therefore I must cast it up.

Exit

Henry VI, part 1

Lord John Talbot

Lord John Talbot (c. 1388–1453) was the principal English military hero
in the latter years of 'The Hundred Years War' between England and
France. The English were in the ascendancy after Henry V's victory at
Agincourt in 1415; but he died in 1422, when his son, Henry VI, was still
a baby and the country was run by a fractious nobility.

The English led by the Earl of Salisbury are besieging the town of
Orléans; Salisbury is badly wounded and almost immediately the
French army led by the newly-emergent Joan of Arc (La Pucelle) attacks.
At this point Talbot has just been in single combat with Joan which
comes to no outright conclusion, but the French army is victorious.

Joan captured Orléans in 1428, which would make Talbot about forty
(she was about sixteen), but I don't see why he cannot be played
younger – providing there's that sense of a battle-hardened soldier.

Historically, it is unlikely that the two ever met.

---

3   *witch* (i.e. Joan)
     Hannibal (A brilliant Carthaginian general, who was supposed to have saved his army by
     driving two thousand oxen with firebrands tied to their horns into the Roman ranks, and
     terrifying the soldiers.)

4   *lists* pleases

5   *noisome* noxious

8   *like to whelps* just like puppies

10 *lions... England's coat* (Lions were a principal part of the English coat of arms.)

11 *soil* country (Some editions have 'style' (meaning 'title') which continues the heraldic sense of
     the previous line.)
     give sheep in lions' stead in place of lions, display sheep (a symbol of cowardice)

12 *treacherous* treacherously

14 *oft-subduèd* often defeated

15 *It will not be* It is hopeless

16 *consented unto* conspired to bring about

Act 1, Scene 5 (Scene 7 in some editions)
Talbot –

1   My thoughts are whirlèd like a potter's wheel;
      I know not where I am nor what I do.
      A witch by fear, not force, like Hannibal,
      Drives back our troops and conquers as she lists.
5   So bees with smoke and doves with noisome stench
      Are from their hives and houses driven away.
      They called us, for our fierceness, English dogs;
      Now, like to whelps, we crying run away.
      A short alarum
      Hark, countrymen: either renew the fight
10   Or tear the lions out of England's coat.
      Renounce your soil; give sheep in lions' stead.
      Sheep run not half so treacherous from the wolf,
      Or horse or oxen from the leopard,
      As you fly from your oft-subduèd slaves.
      Alarum. Here another skirmish
15   It will not be. Retire into your trenches.
      You all consented unto Salisbury's death,
      For none would strike a stroke in his revenge.
      Pucelle is entered into Orléans
      In spite of us or aught that we could do.
                                   Exeunt Soldiers
20   O would I were to die with Salisbury!
      The shame hereof will make me hide my head.
                                            Exit Talbot

Henry VI, part 2

John Hume

John Hume is a corrupt priest who arranges to hire a witch, Margery Jourdain, and two sorcerers, John Southwell and Roger Bolingbroke, for the Duchess of Gloucester (Eleanor Cobham). The Duchess is ambitious and wishes to read the future so that she can prepare – on behalf of her husband – for a possible coup against King Henry VI. She has been checking with Hume that everything is ready, and has just left him on his own.

Historically, there was a Roger Hume arrested for witchcraft, along with the Duchess, but we know nothing else about him – apart from the fact he was pardoned, whereas Shakespeare has him executed. He could be any age you like.

---

2 *Marry* Why, to be sure (a mild swear-word literally meaning, 'by the Virgin Mary')

3 *mum* keep quiet (as in 'keep mum')

4 *asketh* requires

7 *another coast* elsewhere

8 *the rich Cardinal* (i.e. Henry Beaufort, Bishop of Winchester – an enemy of the Duke of Gloucester's and 'rich above the measure of all men... preferring money before friendship')

9 *Duke of Suffolk* (i.e. William de la Pole, an ally of Beaufort's, and a major political intriguer)

11 *aspiring humour* ambitious nature

14 *broker* go-between

17 *call* naming

19 *wrack* ruin

20 *attainture* conviction

21 *Sort how it will* Let things turn out as they will

Act 1, Scene 2
Hume –

1   Hume must make merry with the Duchess' gold;
    Marry, and shall. But how now, Sir John Hume?
    Seal up your lips, and give no words but mum;
    The business asketh silent secrecy.
5   Dame Eleanor gives gold to bring the witch;
    Gold cannot come amiss were she a devil.
    Yet have I gold flies from another coast –
    I dare not say from the rich Cardinal
    And from the great and new-made Duke of Suffolk,
10   Yet I do find it so; for, to be plain,
    They, knowing Dame Eleanor's aspiring humour,
    Have hired me to undermine the Duchess,
    And buzz these conjurations in her brain.
    They say 'A crafty knave does need no broker';
15   Yet am I Suffolk and the Cardinal's broker.
    Hume, if you take not heed, you shall go near
    To call them both a pair of crafty knaves.
    Well, so it stands; and thus, I fear, at last
    Hume's knavery will be the Duchess' wrack,
20   And her attainture will be Humphrey's fall.
    Sort how it will, I shall have gold for all.   *Exit*

Henry VI, part 2

Lieutenant

The Lieutenant (sometimes called a Captain) of a pirate ship. He and his crew have captured another ship and he distributes the prisoners amongst his crew; each crewman is entitled to extract a ransom from his individual prisoner. A crewman Walter Whitmore, who lost an eye in the battle, says he is going to kill his prisoner instead in revenge for his injury. The Lieutenant counsels mercy. However, when he learns that the prisoner is the Duke of Suffolk, the Lieutenant patriotically orders Whitmore to 'Strike off his head' because of the harm the Duke's conspiracies have done England. Suffolk protests and this is the Lieutenant's response.

He could be any age you like above mid-twenties.

––––––––––––––

1   (This is my own version of this line as no two editions have the same; some even have different speakers.)
    Pole (Suffolk's real name, William de la Pole)

2   *kennel* open drain
    sink sewer

6   *lips that kissed the Queen* (Suffolk is passionately in love with Queen Margaret)

7   *good Duke Humphrey* (i.e. Humphrey of Gloucester, King Henry VI's uncle, whose downfall and death were engineered by Suffolk)

8   *Against* Faced with
    senseless unfeeling

10 *the hags of hell* (the Furies, who judged and tortured the wicked after death)

11 *to affy* to affiance (Suffolk arranged the marriage of King Henry and Margaret)

12 *worthless king* (i.e. Reignier, Margaret's impoverished father)

14 *devilish policy* political trickery

15 *Sylla* (Lucius Cornelius Sulla (138–78 B.C.) – notorious for his ruthless persecution of his enemies when he was dictator of Rome.)
    overgorged overfed

16 *gobbets* chunks of raw flesh
    thy mother's (i.e. England's, or Rome in Sulla's case)

17 *Anjou and Maine* (English-held provinces of France which Suffolk promised to Margaret's father in return for his agreement to her marriage with Henry.)

18 *revolting* rebellious
    thorough through

19 *Picardy* (another English-held province of France)

22 *Warwick, and the Nevilles all* (members of the nobility noted for their desire to do good for the country above personal gain)

24 *a guiltless king* (i.e. Richard II, whose deposition and murder by Henry VI began the Lancastrian dynasty)

29 *Advance* Raise up high
    half-faced sun (Both Edward III and Richard II used the device of a sun's rays emerging from the tops of clouds as their personal emblems.)

30 *Invitis nubibus* In spite of clouds

Act 4, Scene 1
Lieutenant –

1   Pole! Sir Poole! Lord!
     Ay, kennel, puddle, sink, whose filth and dirt
     Troubles the silver spring where England drinks;
     Now will I dam up this thy yawning mouth
5   For swallowing the treasure of the realm.
     Thy lips that kissed the Queen shall sweep the ground;
     And thou that smiledst at good Duke Humphrey's death
     Against the senseless winds shalt grin in vain,
     Who in contempt shall hiss at thee again.
10   And wedded be thou to the hags of hell,
     For daring to affy a mighty lord
     Unto the daughter of a worthless king,
     Having neither subject, wealth, nor diadem.
     By devilish policy art thou grown great,
15   And like ambitious Sylla, overgorged
     With gobbets of thy mother's bleeding heart.
     By thee Anjou and Maine were sold to France,
     The false revolting Normans, thorough thee,
     Disdain to call us lord, and Picardy
20   Hath slain their governors, surprised our forts,
     And sent the ragged soldiers, wounded, home.
     The princely Warwick, and the Nevilles all,
     Whose dreadful swords were never drawn in vain,
     As hating thee, are rising up in arms;
25   And now the house of York, thrust from the crown,
     By shameful murder of a guiltless king
     And lofty, proud, encroaching tyranny,
     Burns with revenging fire, whose hopeful colours
     Advance our half-faced sun, striving to shine,
30   Under the which is writ, '*Invitis nubibus*'.
     The commons here in Kent are up in arms;
     And, to conclude, reproach and beggary
     Is crept into the palace of our King,
34   And all by thee. [*To Whitmore*] Away! Convey him hence.

Henry VI, part 2

Jack Cade

Jack Cade (died 1450) was the leader of a rebellion and pretender to the throne of England. Shakespeare has him claim to be of the royal line ('Lord Mortimer') and his revolt is characterised by the preposterous promises he makes to his followers, and its sheer brutality: executing people on the slightest whim. All this viciousness has been commissioned by the Duke of York to give him reason to bring an army into England and suppress the rebels, and take the throne. At this point the rebellion is at its height and Cade is addressing his army when Lord Say, Treasurer of England, is brought before him.

We have no indication of his age, either historically or in the play.

----

1   *say* ((1) kind of silk cloth, (2) pun on Lord Say's name)
    serge heavy wool cloth
    buckram (coarse linen cloth stiffened with glue – used for making stiffened garments, e.g. stage armour)
2   *point-blank* easy range
4   *Basimecu* Kiss my arse (from the French, 'baise mon cul')
    Dolphin (This is 'Dauphin' in some editions.)
5   *presence* present (i.e. the first 'presence' in this line)
6   *besom* broom
9   *the score and the tally* (Crude device for keeping account of debts: a stick was notched to record a debt, then split down the middle, one half being given to the debtor and the other to the creditor; the halves should thus correspond, or tally.)
10 *used* practised
12 *usually* constantly
16 *answer* acquit themselves of
16–17 *because they could not read, thou hast hanged them* (Criminals could be excused from hanging if they claimed 'benefit of clergy', which they could prove by demonstrating that they could read Latin.)
17–18 *only for that cause* for that reason alone
19 *foot-cloth* (Ceremonial hangings used to drape horses, i.e. a sign of some wealth that is especially provocative to Cade and his followers.)

Act 4, Scene 7
Cade –

1   Ah, thou say, thou serge – nay, thou buckram lord! Now art thou within point-blank of our jurisdiction regal. What canst thou answer to my majesty for giving up of Normandy unto Mounsieur Basimecu, the Dolphin of France? Be it known unto

5   thee by these presence, even the presence of Lord Mortimer, that I am the besom that must sweep the court clean of such filth as thou art. Thou hast most traitorously corrupted the youth of the realm in erecting a grammar school; and, whereas before, our forefathers had no other books but the score and the tally, thou

10   hast caused printing to be used; and, contrary to the King his crown and dignity, thou hast built a paper-mill. It will be proved to thy face that thou hast men about thee that usually talk of a noun and a verb, and such abominable words as no Christian ear can endure to hear. Thou hast appointed justices of peace to call

15   poor men before them about matters they were not able to answer. Moreover, thou hast put them in prison; and, because they could not read, thou hast hanged them; when, indeed, only for that cause they have been most worthy to live. Thou dost ride

19   on a foot-cloth, dost thou not?

Henry VI, part 2

Jack Cade

Jack Cade (died 1450) was the leader of a rebellion and pretender to the throne of England. Shakespeare has him claim to be of the royal line ('Lord Mortimer') and his revolt is characterised by the preposterous promises he makes to his followers, and its sheer brutality: executing people on the slightest whim. All this viciousness has been commissioned by the Duke of York to give him reason to bring an army into England and suppress the rebels, and take the throne. The rebellion is short-lived; the rebels are persuaded to give up in return for free pardons, leaving Cade a fugitive. He is here in a garden reflecting on his situation.

We have no indication of his age, either historically or in the play.

---

2   *ready to famish* all-but starving
3   *laid for me* circulated with warrants for my arrest
4   *lease* extension
5   *stay* (i.e. in hiding)
    o'er (This is 'on' in some editions.)
7   *sallet* (1) salad, (2) light round helmet (also lines 9, 10 and 13)
7–8 *cool a man's stomach* satisfy a man's hunger
10 *brown bill* bronzed pike carried by constables

44

Act 4, Scene 9
Cade –

Enter Jack Cade

1 Fie on ambitions! Fie on myself that have a sword and yet am ready to famish! These five days have I hid me in these woods and durst not peep out, for all the country is laid for me. But now am I so hungry that if I might have a lease of my life for
5 a thousand years, I could stay no longer. Wherefore o'er a brick wall have I climbed into this garden to see if I can eat grass or pick a sallet another while, which is not amiss to cool a man's stomach this hot weather. And I think this word 'sallet' was born to do me good; for many a time, but for a
10 sallet, my brain-pan had been cleft with a brown bill; and many a time, when I have been dry, and bravely marching, it hath served me instead of a quart-pot to drink in; and now the
13 word 'sallet' must serve me to feed on.

Henry VI, part 2

John Clifford ('Young Clifford')

John Clifford ('Young Clifford') (c. 1435–1461) is the son of Lord Thomas Clifford – both were supporters of King Henry VI against the claims of the Duke of York. York has just returned from Ireland to claim the throne and the first battle is fought at St. Albans (1455). The battle goes badly for the King's forces and Clifford's father is killed by York. Almost immediately Young Clifford arrives on the scene, at first not seeing his father's body.

In *Henry VI, part 3* he goes on to extract his bloody vengeance against York.

I have cut the final five lines of this speech to make it a better length for audition.

----

1 *on the rout* in chaotic retreat
2 *frames* creates
5 *frozen* (i.e. with fear)
   part side
11 *premised* preordained
13 *general trumpet* trumpet which summons everybody to account
14 *Particularities* Details
   petty sounds trivial talk
15 *ordained* destined
16 *lose* spend
17 *advisèd age* wise old age
18 *reverence* venerable old age
   chair-days last days
21 *stony* without pity
23 *as the dew to fire* (Water drops sprinkled on to fire were supposed to make it burn more fiercely.)
24 *reclaims* subdues
25 *oil and flax* (i.e. provoking his 'fire' to burn more fiercely)
28 *gobbets* chunks of raw flesh
29 *Medea, Absyrtus* (In Greek mythology Medea murdered her younger brother, Absyrtus, and strewed the pieces of his corpse behind her so that her father, by picking them up, would be delayed in his pursuit of her.)
30 *fame* reputation

Act 5, Scene 2 (Scene 3 in some editions)
Young Clifford –

Alarums, then enter Young Clifford

1   Shame and confusion! All is on the rout;
     Fear frames disorder, and disorder wounds
     Where it should guard. O war, thou son of hell,
     Whom angry heavens do make their minister,
5   Throw in the frozen bosoms of our part
     Hot coals of vengeance! Let no soldier fly!
     He that is truly dedicate to war
     Hath no self-love; nor he that loves himself
     Hath not essentially, but by circumstance,
10   The name of valour. [*He sees his father's body*] O, let the
       vile world end,
     And the premised flames of the last day
     Knit earth and heaven together.
     Now let the general trumpet blow his blast,
     Particularities and petty sounds
15   To cease! Wast thou ordained, dear father,
     To lose thy youth in peace, and to achieve
     The silver livery of advisèd age,
     And in thy reverence and thy chair-days, thus
     To die in ruffian battle? Even at this sight
20   My heart is turned to stone, and while 'tis mine
     It shall be stony. York not our old men spares;
     No more will I their babes. Tears virginal
     Shall be to me even as the dew to fire,
     And beauty that the tyrant oft reclaims
25   Shall to my flaming wrath be oil and flax.
     Henceforth I will not have to do with pity;
     Meet I an infant of the house of York,
     Into as many gobbets will I cut it
     As wild Medea young Absyrtus did.
30   In cruelty will I seek out my fame.

Henry VIII

Duke of Buckingham

The Duke of Buckingham, Edward Stafford (1478–1521) was the son of Richard III's closest crony (until his execution), Henry Stafford; he was also a distant relative of the King's. Edward seems to be much more honest and straightforward than his father, even somewhat foolish in openly expressing his opinions. He is here talking to like-minded friends, the Duke of Norfolk and Lord Abergavenny (also his father-in-law) about Cardinal Wolsey's misuse of his power. Wolsey was chief adviser to Henry VIII and helped to organise the famous meeting between Henry VIII and Francis I of France at 'The Field of Cloth of Gold' in 1520 – the aim of which was to bring about a long-term non-aggression treaty between England and France, and eventually throughout Europe. However high-minded this may sound Wolsey was also feathering his own nest. Buckingham and his aristocratic friends also disliked Wolsey because he came from the middle-classes and had displaced the nobility as the chief source of advice to the King.

Later in the play Buckingham is found guilty of treason and on his way to execution publicly forgives his enemies and wishes the King well.

He is about forty at this time.

---

2 *articles o' th' combination* terms of the treaty (i.e. that between Henry VIII and Francis I of France in June 1520 – at 'The Field of Cloth of Gold')

5 *count-Cardinal* (Wolsey was not so-ennobled, Buckingham is emphasising Wolsey's presumption of powers he shouldn't have. This is 'Court-Cardinal' in some editions.)

9 *dam* bitch (i.e. female parent of an animal)
   Charles the Emperor (Holy Roman Emperor Charles V (also King Charles I of Spain) – secular head of the Roman Catholic Church.)

10 *the Queen his aunt* (Katherine of Aragon (Henry's wife at this point) was sister of Joanna, mother of Charles.)

11 *colour* pretext

12 *whisper* speak with in secret

16 *Privily he* Secretly he (This is sometimes 'He privily' or simply 'Privily' in some editions.)

17 *trow* believe

25 *buy and sell* betray for money

Act 1, Scene 1
Buckingham –

1   Pray give me favour, sir. This cunning Cardinal,
The articles o' th' combination drew
As himself pleased, and they were ratified
As he cried 'Thus let be', to as much end
5   As give a crutch to th' dead. But our count-Cardinal
Has done this, and 'tis well for worthy Wolsey,
Who cannot err, he did it. Now this follows –
Which, as I take it, is a kind of puppy
To th' old dam, treason – Charles the Emperor,
10   Under pretence to see the Queen his aunt –
For 'twas indeed his colour, but he came
To whisper Wolsey – here makes visitation.
His fears were that the interview betwixt
England and France might through their amity
15   Breed him some prejudice, for from this league
Peeped harms that menaced him. Privily he
Deals with our Cardinal and, as I trow –
Which I do well, for I am sure the Emperor
Paid ere he promised, whereby his suit was granted
20   Ere it was asked – but when the way was made,
And paved with gold, the Emperor thus desired
That he would please to alter the King's course
And break the foresaid peace. Let the King know,
As soon he shall by me, that thus the Cardinal
25   Does buy and sell his honour as he pleases,
And for his own advantage.

Henry VIII

Cardinal Thomas Wolsey

Cardinal Thomas Wolsey (c. 1475-1530) was the highly-intelligent son of a prosperous livestock dealer and wool merchant. His intelligence and drive gained him rapid promotion, becoming Henry VIII's chaplain and then on to be Archbishop of York, a Cardinal, Lord Chancellor and Henry's chief adviser – virtually governing the country. He introduced some significant judicial reforms and was a statesman of international renown, but also made himself deeply unpopular with a number of people through his use of power for his own gain. Shakespeare's Wolsey starts the play as a greedy, arrogant and corrupt politician; but after his fall from power he shows profound contrition for his misdeeds.

In 1528 Henry ordered Wolsey to see to his divorce from Katherine, his Queen of twenty years – a very difficult task under the rules of the Roman Catholic Church. In this scene the divorce petition is being heard and Katherine has just turned on Wolsey accusing him of having 'blown this coal betwixt my lord and me' (i.e. stirred dissent between Henry and herself) and utterly refusing to be judged by him, whom she 'holds my most malicious foe, and think not / At all a friend to truth'. This is his response.

----

3   *stood to* supported
6   *spleen* malice
9   *consistory* College of Cardinals
13 *gainsay my deed* deny what you say I have done
    wound punish
14 *worthily* rightly
15 *truth* credibility
16 *free of your report* innocent of your charge
17 *your wrong* (free of) the wrong you have done me (in accusing me of wrong-doing)
18 *It* The solution
20 *in* about

Henry VIII

Act 2, Scene 4
Wolsey –

1   I do profess
        You speak not like yourself, who ever yet
        Have stood to charity, and displayed th' effects
        Of disposition gentle and of wisdom
5   O'er-topping woman's power. Madam, you do me wrong.
        I have no spleen against you, nor injustice
        For you or any. How far I have proceeded,
        Or how far further shall, is warranted
        By a commission from the consistory,
10   Yea, the whole consistory of Rome. You charge me
        That I 'have blown this coal'. I do deny it.
        The King is present. If it be known to him
        That I gainsay my deed, how may he wound,
        And worthily, my falsehood – yea, as much
15   As you have done my truth. If he know
        That I am free of your report, he knows
        I am not of your wrong. Therefore in him
        It lies to cure me, and the cure is to
        Remove these thoughts from you. The which before
20   His highness shall speak in, I do beseech
        You, gracious madam, to unthink your speaking,
22   And to say so no more.

King John

Prince Arthur

Prince Arthur (1187–1203) was the son of King John's older brother, Geoffrey, and a rival claimant to the throne. Arthur's cause is promoted by Constance, his mother, and supported by King Philip II of France. Arthur has not long been captured by his uncle, and is in the custody of Hubert de Burgh, who has just shown Arthur a warrant which commands that his eyes be burnt out with hot irons. The two have become quite friendly and Arthur challenges Hubert's resolve with this speech.

Historically Arthur was sixteen at this point but Shakespeare implies that he is significantly younger.

———————

2   *knit* tied
   handkerchief (This is 'handkercher' in some editions.)
3   *wrought* worked (i.e. embroidered)
4   *ask it you again* ask it back from you
6   *watchful* progressing
7   *Still and anon* Regularly (without stopping)
   heavy dreary
8   *grief* pain
9   *good love* kind deed
10 *lyen* lain (This is 'lien' and 'lain' in most editions, but I think this spelling best evokes what's necessary for the metre.)
12 *at your sick service* at your service when you were sick
14 *an if you will* if you wish to

Act 4, Scene 1
Arthur –

1   Have you the heart? When your head did but ache
      I knit my handkerchief about your brows –
      The best I had, a princess wrought it me –
      And I did never ask it you again;
5   And with my hand at midnight held your head,
      And like the watchful minutes to the hour
      Still and anon cheered up the heavy time,
      Saying 'What lack you?' and 'Where lies your grief?'
      Or 'What good love may I perform for you?'
10   Many a poor man's son would have lyen still
      And ne'er have spoke a loving word to you,
      But you at your sick service had a prince.
      Nay, you may think my love was crafty love,
      And call it cunning: do, an if you will.
15   If heaven be pleased that you must use me ill,
      Why then you must. Will you put out mine eyes –
      These eyes that never did, nor never shall,
18   So much as frown on you?

Love's Labour's Lost

Don Adriano de Armado

Don Adriano de Armado is a comically pedantic, verbose, 'fantastical' and pompous Spaniard, who claims to be a soldier. He is a man very much in love with himself; he is also in love with Jaquenetta, a young dairy-maid. He has just seen her and she has been somewhat cool with him, but he is oblivious. Left alone he reflects on his love for her.

Beneath his absurd posturings there is a real person, and later when he tries to pass off his lack of a shirt he is revealed as a rather pathetic figure. He could be any age from mid-twenties upwards.

---

1   *affect* love
3   *be forsworn* break my oath
    argument proof
5   *familiar* attendant evil spirit
8   *butt-shaft* unbarbed arrow (These were used in training and hit hard but were easily extracted.)
9   *much odds* powerful
10 *Spaniard's rapier* (The rapier was regarded as particularly Spanish.)
    The first and second cause (The 'causes' which would incite a gentleman to fight a duel, i.e. (1) the accusation of a capital crime and (2) a matter of honour.)
11 *passado* forward thrust with the sword (a foot being advanced at the same time)
    he (i.e. Cupid, and 'his' in line 12)
    duello code of duelling
15 *extemporal god of rhyme* god of impromptu poetry
    turn sonnet become a writer of sonnets
16 *folio* (large format book)

Act 1, Scene 2
Armado –

1   I do affect the very ground, which is base – where her shoe,
       which is baser – guided by her foot, which is basest – doth
       tread. I shall be forsworn – which is a great argument of
       falsehood – if I love. And how can that be true love which
5   is falsely attempted? Love is a familiar; Love is a devil;
       there is no evil angel but Love. Yet was Samson so tempted,
       and he had an excellent strength; yet was Solomon so
       seduced, and he had a very good wit. Cupid's butt-shaft is
       too hard for Hercules' club, and therefore too much odds
10   for a Spaniard's rapier. The first and second cause will not
       serve my turn; the passado he respects not, the duello he
       regards not. His disgrace is to be called boy, but his glory is
       to subdue men. Adieu, valour; rust, rapier; be still, drum:
       for your manager is in love; yea, he loveth. Assist me, some
15   extemporal god of rhyme, for I am sure I shall turn sonnet.
       Devise, wit; write, pen; for I am for whole volumes in folio.
                                                              Exit

Love's Labour's Lost

Boyet

Boyet is a lord, and adviser, attending the Princess of France. She is on a diplomatic mission to the King of Navarre (now part in France and part in Spain). He is a smooth courtier who delights in trading witticisms with his mistress and her three attendant ladies; he is also a messenger and a sharp observer of human behaviour. The Princess's party has recently arrived in Navarre only to learn that the King has vowed to exclude women from his court for three years in order that he (and his courtiers) may pursue scholarship so that 'Navarre shall be the wonder of the world'. The King and his courtiers arrive and there is some formal diplomatic discussion, but it becomes clear that the men are somewhat taken by the ladies. The King's party leave, but the courtiers individually return to ask Boyet about the Princess' ladies. Boyet then gives this summary of his perception of the King's real feelings to the Princess.

He could be almost any age from mid-twenties upwards.

I have cut two short lines from the Princess to construct this speech.

---

2   *still rhetoric* silent eloquence
      disclosed with eyes revealed by the (look in the) eyes
4   *'affected'* overwhelmed by love
5–6 *all his behaviours did make their retire* all his faculties retreated
6   *To the court of his eye* To concentrate on what he saw
      thorough through
7–8 *agate with your print impressed* agate engraved with an image of yourself (Agates were often set into lovers' rings.)
8   *Proud with his form* Possessed by the Princess's image ('impressed' on his 'heart')
9   *all impatient to speak and not see* frustrated because he is only able to speak to, not see (the Princess)
11   *that sense* (i.e. eyesight)
      repair resort
12   *only looking* only by looking
14   *crystal* crystal-glass
15   *tend'ring* offering
      glassed enclosed in ('crystal') glass
16   *point* provoke
17   *margin* (In Elizabethan books textual notes were often printed in the margins. This is 'margent' in some editions.)
19   *Aquitaine* (Region of France, and part of the diplomatic negotiations.)
20   *An* If

Act 2, Scene 1
Boyet –

1   If my observation, which very seldom lies,
By the heart's still rhetoric disclosed with eyes,
Deceive me not now, Navarre is infected
With that which we lovers entitle 'affected'.
5   Why, all his behaviours did make their retire
To the court of his eye, peeping thorough desire.
His heart like an agate with your print impressed,
Proud with his form, in his eye pride expressed.
His tongue, all impatient to speak and not see,
10   Did stumble with haste in his eyesight to be.
All senses to that sense did make their repair,
To feel only looking on fairest of fair.
Methought all his senses were locked in his eye,
As jewels in crystal, for some prince to buy;
15   Who, tend'ring their own worth from where they were
      glassed,
Did point you to buy them, along as you passed.
His face's own margin did quote such amazes
That all eyes saw his eyes enchanted with gazes.
I'll give you Aquitaine and all that is his,
20   An you give him for my sake but one loving kiss.

Love's Labour's Lost

Mote

Mote (sometimes 'Moth') is a young page to Don Adriano de Armado, a pedantic and pompous Spaniard. Mote spends the play ridiculing his master, subtly to his face and blatantly behind his back. Armado is infatuated with Jacquenetta and Mote has just suggested that his master might win her with a 'French brawl' (which is a dance) – Armado takes this to mean a brawl (i.e. a quarrel) in French; Mote puts him right with this speech.

Mote can be played by either a man or a woman.

———————————

1   *jig off a tune* sing some jig-like (bright and lively) tune
2   *canary* (lively Spanish dance)
3–6 *sigh... love* (All these are demonstrations of love.)
4   *sometime* at times
7   *penthouse-like* like a projecting roof (i.e. making him look melancholy)
8   *thin-belly doublet* doublet covering a thin belly (suggesting someone wasted through pining for love)
9   *after* in the style of (We do not know of any specific 'old painting' that Mote refers to.)
10–11 *snip and away* a snatch and then on to another
11   *complements* proper manners
     humours moods
12   *betray* attract
     nice coy
     be betrayed not be attracted (and 'feel let down')
13   *of note* of distinction
13–14 *do you note me?* (There are several variations on this line in different editions; this version seems the most appropriate to me.)
14   *affected* inclined
     to these (i.e. 'complements and humours')

Act 3, Scene 1
Mote –

1   No, my complete master; but to jig off a tune at the
tongue's end, canary to it with your feet, humour it with
turning up your eyelids, sigh a note and sing a note,
sometime through the throat as if you swallowed love
5   with singing love, sometime through the nose as if you
snuffed up love by smelling love; with your hat
penthouse-like o'er the shop of your eyes; with your arms
crossed on your thin-belly doublet like a rabbit on a spit;
or your hands in your pocket like a man after the old
10   painting; and keep not too long in one tune, but a snip
and away. These are complements, these are humours;
these betray nice wenches, that would be betrayed
without these; and make them men of note – do you note
14   me? – that most are affected to these.

Love's Labour's Lost

Don Adriano de Armado

Don Adriano de Armado is a comically pedantic, verbose, 'fantastical' and pompous Spaniard, who claims to be a soldier; he is a man very much in love with himself. He is here with his two equally absurd friends (Nathaniel, the curate, and Holofernes, the schoolmaster), and has just announced that the King has asked him to arrange a welcome for the newly arrived Princess of France.

Beneath his absurd posturings there is a real person, and later when he tries to pass off his lack of a shirt he is revealed as a rather pathetic figure.

He could be any age from mid-twenties upwards.

---

1 *familiar* intimate
2 *inward* private
3 *let it pass* never mind about that
   remember thy courtesy remember your manners (i.e. those appropriate to royalty, bowing and doffing one's hat))
4 *apparel thy head* put on your hat
9 *excrement* outgrowth (e.g. hair or nails or as here his moustache)
10 *I recount no fable* I tell you no tales
13 *The very all of all* The upshot
15 *sweet chuck* sweet chick (A very familiar term of affection; as in 'sweetheart' above.)
16 *ostentation* spectacular display
   antic fantastical entertainment (in which the actors wore extraordinary costumes)

Act 5, Scene 1
Armado –

1   Sir, the King is a noble gentleman, and my familiar, I do
       assure ye, very good friend. For what is inward between
       us, let it pass. I do beseech thee, remember thy courtesy; I
       beseech thee, apparel thy head. And, among other
5   important and most serious designs, and of great import
       indeed, too – but let that pass, for I must tell thee it will
       please his grace, by the world, sometime to lean upon my
       poor shoulder and with his royal finger thus dally with
       my excrement, with my mustachio – but, sweetheart, let
10   that pass. By the world, I recount no fable. Some certain
       special honours it pleaseth his greatness to impart to
       Armado, a soldier, a man of travel, that hath seen the
       world – but let that pass. The very all of all is – but,
       sweetheart, I do implore secrecy – that the King would
15   have me present the Princess, sweet chuck, with some
       delightful ostentation, or show, or pageant, or antic, or
       firework. Now, understanding that the curate and your
       sweet self are good at such eruptions and sudden
       breaking-out of mirth, as it were, I have acquainted you
20   withal to the end to crave your assistance.

Love's Labour's Lost

Boyet

Boyet is a lord, and adviser, attending the Princess of France. She is on a diplomatic mission to the King of Navarre (now part in France and part in Spain). He is a smooth courtier who delights in trading witticisms with his mistress and her three attendant ladies; he is also a messenger and a sharp observer of human behaviour. The Princess' party has recently arrived in Navarre only to learn that the King has vowed to exclude women from his court for three years in order that he (and his courtiers) may pursue scholarship so that 'Navarre shall be the wonder of the world'. However, after a brief diplomatic meeting, the King (and three of his courtiers) set about pursuing the lady that each is attracted to. The men become faintly ludicrous in their attempts at wooing and here Boyet is describing to the Princess and her ladies, what he has heard the men planning next.

Boyet could be almost any age from mid-twenties upwards.

———————

4   *might* could
    addressed approaching
7   *overhear* hear over
10 *conned his embassage* learned his message (i.e. one entrusted to an ambassador)
13 *made a doubt* expressed fear that
14 *Presence majestical* Regal presence
    put him out make him tongue-tied
16 *audaciously* boldly
19 *clapped him on the shoulder* patted him on the back (in approval)
21 *One rubbed his elbow* (An itching elbow was thought to be a sign of satisfaction.)
    fleered grinned
23 *his finger and his thumb* snaps his fingers (in exuberance of spirits)
24 *Via* Come on
26 *turned on the toe* pirouetted
29 *spleen ridiculous* hysterical laughter
30 *solemn* melancholy

Love's Labour's Lost

Act 5, Scene 2
Boyet –

1   Under the cool shade of a sycamore
I thought to close mine eyes some half an hour,
When lo, to interrupt my purposed rest
Toward that shade I might behold addressed
5   The King and his companions. Warily
I stole into a neighbour thicket by
And overheard what you shall overhear:
That, by and by, disguised they will be here.
Their herald is a pretty knavish page
10   That well by heart hath conned his embassage.
Action and accent did they teach him there:
'Thus must thou speak', and 'thus thy body bear'.
And ever and anon they made a doubt
Presence majestical would put him out,
15   'For', quoth the King, 'an angel shalt thou see;
Yet fear not thou, but speak audaciously.'
The boy replied, 'An angel is not evil;
I should have feared her had she been a devil.'
With that all laughed and clapped him on the shoulder,
20   Making the bold wag by their praises bolder.
One rubbed his elbow thus, and fleered, and swore
A better speech was never spoke before.
Another, with his finger and his thumb,
Cried '*Via*, we will do 't, come what will come!'
25   The third he capered and cried, 'All goes well!'
The fourth turned on the toe and down he fell.
With that they all did tumble on the ground
With such a zealous laughter, so profound,
That in this spleen ridiculous appears,
30   To check their folly, passion's solemn tears.

The Merchant of Venice

Gratiano

Gratiano is one of a group of young men who are friends of Antonio (the 'Merchant' of the title) and his close friend, Bassanio. He is a crude, garrulous, volatile and frivolous companion. As Bassanio puts it, 'Gratiano speaks an infinite deal of nothing' and 'Thou art too wild, too rude, and bold of voice'. His manner even turns ugly later in the trial scene (Act 4, Scene 1), where he crudely baits the desperate Shylock. At this point, accompanied by Bassanio and Lorenzo (another friend), he has just bumped into Antonio. Gratiano comments, 'You look not well'; Antonio says he is 'sad' and this is Gratiano's response.

----

2   *let old wrinkles come*   create wrinkles (like those of old age)

3–4   *heart cool with mortifying groans*   (It was believed that sighs and groans drained blood from the heart, the seat of love.)

6   *grandsire cut in alabaster*   grandfather's tombstone (Alabaster was frequently used for these as it is easily carved.)

7   *when he wakes*   when he should stay awake (to carry on having fun)

       jaundice   yellowing of the skin (caused by obstruction of the bile, and thought to be caused by negative emotions)

10   *sort*   kind

11   *cream and mantle*   acquire a fixed (and sour) expression (literally, grow a scum – on a still liquid surface)

12   *wilful stillness entertain*   maintain an obstinate silence

13   *dressed in an opinion*   acquire a reputation for

14   *conceit*   understanding

20   *damn those ears*   (According to St Matthew, 5.22: 'whosoever shall say, Thou fool, shall be in danger of hell fire'.)

23   *fish not*   don't look for (friendship)

24   *gudgeon*   (a fresh-water fish, easily caught; figuratively, a gullible person)

26   *exhortation*   sermon

Act 1, Scene 1
Gratiano –

1   Let me play the fool.
     With mirth and laughter let old wrinkles come,
     And let my liver rather heat with wine
     Than my heart cool with mortifying groans.
5   Why should a man whose blood is warm within
     Sit like his grandsire cut in alabaster,
     Sleep when he wakes, and creep into the jaundice
     By being peevish? I tell thee what, Antonio –
     I love thee, and 'tis my love that speaks –
10   There are a sort of men whose visages
     Do cream and mantle like a standing pond,
     And do a wilful stillness entertain
     With purpose to be dressed in an opinion
     Of wisdom, gravity, profound conceit,
15   As who should say 'I am Sir Oracle,
     And when I ope my lips, let no dog bark'.
     O my Antonio, I do know of these
     That therefore only are reputed wise
     For saying nothing, when I am very sure,
20   If they should speak, would almost damn those ears
     Which, hearing them, would call their brothers fools.
     I'll tell thee more of this another time.
     But fish not with this melancholy bait
     For this fool gudgeon, this opinion.
25   Come, good Lorenzo. Fare ye well a while,
     I'll end my exhortation after dinner.

The Merchant of Venice

Antonio

Antonio is the 'Merchant' of the title. He borrows money from Shylock to help his impoverished friend Bassanio in order that he might present a suitable appearance as a suitor to the wealthy Portia. Antonio's money is all tied up in trading ships, currently at sea, so they resort to Shylock, the money-lender. Antonio is completely opposed to the idea of lending money 'upon advantage' (with interest), so Shylock comes up with the idea that instead of interest Antonio will only be liable to a 'forfeit' of 'an equal pound / Of your fair flesh' if he doesn't repay the loan within three months. Antonio takes this as a joke ('My ships come home a month before the day') and agrees.

Later, news comes through that all Antonio's ships have been lost at sea, and he is brought to trial to answer Shylock's demand that the 'forfeit' be paid in full. At this point all seems lost and Antonio has just been asked if he has 'anything to say'.

Antonio's relationship with his circle of male friends, especially Bassanio, is sexually ambiguous. Unlike the others he shows no overt interest in women; another of the circle comments, 'I think he only loves the world for him' (i.e. Bassanio); and in a letter to Bassanio, when he thinks his bond is 'forfeit', he asks to see him before he dies – you have to decide on the exact nature of his 'love' for Bassanio.

We are not given any real indication of his age, but he is well-established amongst the merchant class. I suggest he could be anywhere from late twenties upwards.

———————

5   *still her use* regularly her habit
11 *process* (i.e. the legal one)
13 *loved* (i.e. as a close friend, but see above)
15 *Repent but you* Grieve only
16 *he* (i.e. Antonio)

Act 4, Scene 1
Antonio –

1   I am armed and well prepared.
       Give me your hand, Bassanio; fare you well.
       Grieve not that I am fall'n to this for you,
       For herein Fortune shows herself more kind
5   Than is her custom. It is still her use
       To let the wretched man outlive his wealth,
       To view with hollow eye and wrinkled brow
       An age of poverty; from which ling'ring penance
       Of such misery doth she cut me off.
10   Commend me to your honourable wife.
       Tell her the process of Antonio's end.
       Say how I loved you. Speak me fair in death,
       And when the tale is told, bid her be judge
       Whether Bassanio had not once a love.
15   Repent but you that you shall lose your friend,
       And he repents not that he pays your debt;
       For if the Jew do cut but deep enough,
18   I'll pay it instantly, with all my heart.

The Merry Wives of Windsor

Frank Ford

Frank Ford is a citizen of Windsor and husband to Alice Ford, one of the 'Merry Wives'. He hears a story that the famously fat and debauched Sir John Falstaff is trying to seduce his wife (and Mistress Page, wife of his friend, George Page). Whilst Page dismisses the idea, Ford decides to investigate. He disguises himself as 'Master Brook' to elicit more information from Falstaff, who tells him, 'I shall be with her between ten and eleven'. Falstaff has just left Page alone.

Although he is generally played older, he could be as young as late twenties.

---

1   *epicurean* lecherous
2   *improvident* baseless
7–8 *stand under the adoption of abominable terms* run the risk of being called detestable names
9–10 *'Amaimon'... 'Lucifer'... 'Barbason'* (Devils' names)
11   *additions* titles
     wittol tamely accepting cuckold
13   *secure* over-confident
14–15 *Fleming... Welshman.. Irishman* (Proverbially, each was over-fond of these respective items.)
16   *aqua-vitae* spirits (such as brandy and whisky; literally, 'water of life'.)
     walk exercise (a horse, at walking pace)
19 & 20 *effect* carry it out
20   *God* (This is 'Heaven' in some editions.)
21   *detect* expose
23   *God's my life* (This is 'Fie, fie, fie!' in some editions.)

Act 2, Scene 2
Ford –

1   What a damned epicurean rascal is this! My heart is ready
to crack with impatience. Who says this is improvident
jealousy? My wife hath sent to him, the hour is fixed, the
match is made. Would any man have thought this? See the
5   hell of having a false woman! My bed shall be abused, my
coffers ransacked, my reputation gnawn at, and I shall not
only receive this villainous wrong, but stand under the
adoption of abominable terms, and by him that does me
this wrong. Terms! Names! 'Amaimon' sounds well;
10   'Lucifer', well; 'Barbason', well: yet they are devils'
additions, the names of fiends. But 'cuckold', 'wittol'!
'Cuckold' – the devil himself hath not such a name. Page is
an ass, a secure ass. He will trust his wife, he will not be
jealous. I will rather trust a Fleming with my butter, Parson
15   Hugh the Welshman with my cheese, an Irishman with my
aqua-vitae bottle, or a thief to walk my ambling gelding,
than my wife with herself. Then she plots, then she
ruminates, then she devises. And what they think in their
hearts they may effect, they will break their hearts but they
20   will effect. God be praised for my jealousy! Eleven o'clock
the hour. I will prevent this, detect my wife, be revenged on
Falstaff, and laugh at Page. I will about it. Better three
hours too soon than a minute too late. God's my life:
24   cuckold, cuckold, cuckold!   *Exit*

Much Ado About Nothing

Don John

Don John is the illegitimate brother of the prince, Don Pedro and has a large chip on his shoulder. Before the play he has rebelled against his brother and been defeated, but the prince forgives him. At the beginning of the play he arrives with his brother at the house of Leonato, governor of Messina – in amongst all the hearty welcomes he says only one line: 'I thank you. I am not of many words, but I thank you'. In this scene his 'follower', Conrad, has been trying to persuade him to cheer up, and endure his sufferings patiently, in order to preserve his newly restored position in Don Pedro's court. He is generally played in his twenties, but he could be almost any age above this.

This is two speeches run together.

———————————————

1–2 *born under Saturn* (i.e. cold and gloomy)
2 *moral medicine* moralising comfort
3 *mortifying mischief* deadly misfortune
4–5 *eat when I have stomach* eat when I please
6 *tend on* attend to
7 *claw no man in his humour* pander to nobody's wishes
8 *canker* wild rose (considered a weed)
   his (i.e. Don Pedro's)
   grace favour
9 *blood* temperament
   fashion a carriage pretend a (pleasant) mode of behaviour
12 *trusted with a muzzle* trusted as much as a muzzled dog
13 *enfranchised with a clog* given my freedom with shackles (A 'clog' was a weight attached to an animal to restrict its movements.)
   decreed made up my mind

Act 1, Scene 3
Don John –

1   I wonder that thou – being, as thou say'st thou art, born under Saturn – goest about to apply a moral medicine to a mortifying mischief. I cannot hide what I am: I must be sad when I have cause, and smile at no man's jests; eat when I
5   have stomach, and wait for no man's leisure; sleep when I am drowsy, and tend on no man's business; laugh when I am merry, and claw no man in his humour. I had rather be a canker in a hedge than a rose in his grace, and it better fits my blood to be disdained of all than to fashion a carriage
10   to rob love from any. In this, though I cannot be said to be a flattering honest man, it must not be denied but I am a plain-dealing villain. I am trusted with a muzzle and enfranchised with a clog; therefore I have decreed not to sing in my cage. If I had my mouth, I would bite; if I had
15   my liberty, I would do my liking. In the mean time, let me be that I am, and seek not to alter me.

Much Ado About Nothing

Claudio

Claudio is a gallant young nobleman about to marry Hero, daughter of Leonato, governor of Messina. However, the night before the wedding, he and his mentor, Don Pedro, think they see her at her bedroom window talking affectionately with another man. Claudio swears that he will 'before the whole congregation, shame her with what he saw o'ernight, and send her home again without a husband'. The wedding ceremony has just begun when he interrupts the proceedings.

It turns out that the woman he saw at Hero's window was one of her waiting women and that he has been deliberately tricked into thinking it was Hero. He may seem very stupid to have been taken in like this, but the more experienced Don Pedro is likewise duped. More importantly, Claudio is young, inexperienced and very much in love. He believes that she has cruelly betrayed him and his revenge must be equal.

This is several speeches put together, and I have changed a few words to help it make sense in isolation from the play.

---

1   *Stand thee by* Stand aside

     by your leave if I may so call you

5   *counterpoise* be equal to

11 *authority* credibility

13 *modest evidence* evidence of modesty

14 *witness* bear witness to

17 *luxurious* lustful

20 *approved* proven

23 *extenuate* excuse

     forehand sin (i.e. premarital sex)

25 *large* immodest

Act 4, Scene 1
Claudio –

1   Stand thee by, Friar. [*To Leonato*] Father, by your leave:
        You will with free and unconstrainèd soul
        Give me this maid, your daughter;
        But what have I to give you back, whose worth
5   May counterpoise this rich and precious gift?
        Nothing, unless I render her again.
        There, Leonato, take her back again.
        Give not this rotten orange to your friend;
        She's but the sign and semblance of her honour.
10   Behold how like a maid she blushes here!
        O, what authority and show of truth
        Can cunning sin cover itself withal!
        Comes not that blood as modest evidence
        To witness simple virtue? Would you not swear –
15   All you that see her – that she were a maid,
        By these exterior shows? But she is none.
        She knows the heat of a luxurious bed;
        Her blush is guiltiness, not modesty.
        I wish not to be married,
20   Not to knit my soul to an approved wanton.
        I know what you would say. If I have known her,
        You will say she did embrace me as a husband,
        And so extenuate the forehand sin.
        No, Leonato,
25   I never tempted her with word too large,
        But as a brother to his sister showed
27   Bashful sincerity and comely love.

Pericles

Pericles

Pericles is Prince of Tyre (now in southern Lebanon). He has heard the stories about the King of Antioch's daughter, and resolves – 'Emboldened with the glory of her praise' – to attempt to solve the 'riddle' that is the passport to her hand in marriage. Any suitor who attempts this and fails is executed. Immediately on reading the 'riddle' Pericles realises that its solution reveals the King and his daughter's relationship is incestuous. He declines to give his answer, but clearly hints that he knows the implications. The King decides to humour him and gives him forty days to come up with the solution. Pericles has just been left on his own and is contemplating his situation.

We are given no real indication of his age, but he could be as young as late teens at this point.

There is strong suspicion that this is part of the play written by George Wilkins or another contemporary writer, but very few people will worry about this for audition.

———————————

1   *seem* pretend
3   *sight* outward appearance
7   *Where* However
8   *untimely* (This is 'uncomely' in some editions, which seems to me a bit weak; 'untimely' more conveys the grossness of the incest.)
15 *Blush* Who blush
16 *shun* (This is either 'schew' (i.e. eschew) or 'shew' (i.e. show) in other editions.)
20 *targets* shields
     put off avert
21 *cropped* cut off
     clear free from suspicion

Act 1, Scene 1
Pericles –

1   How courtesy would seem to cover sin
When what is done is like an hypocrite,
The which is good in nothing but in sight.
If it be true that I interpret false,
5   Then were it certain you were not so bad
As with foul incest to abuse your soul;
Where now you're both a father and a son
By your uncomely claspings with your child –
Which pleasures fits a husband, not a father –
10   And she, an eater of her mother's flesh,
By the defiling of her parents' bed;
And both like serpents are, who though they feed
On sweetest flowers, yet they poison breed.
Antioch, farewell, for wisdom sees those men
15   Blush not in actions blacker than the night
Will shun no course to keep them from the light.
One sin, I know, another doth provoke;
Murder's as near to lust as flame to smoke.
Poison and treason are the hands of sin,
20   Ay, and the targets to put off the shame.
Then, lest my life be cropped to keep you clear,
22   By flight I'll shun the danger which I fear.   *Exit*

Richard II

Thomas Mowbray, Duke of Norfolk

Thomas Mowbray, Duke of Norfolk (c. 1365–1400) is accused at the beginning of the play by Henry Bolingbroke, Duke of Hereford (and later King Henry IV) of, amongst other things, murdering the Duke of Gloucester, the King's (and also Bolingbroke's) uncle. Mowbray protests his innocence and demands trial by combat, with Bolingbroke. In this scene Richard has stopped the combat just before it can begin and ordered that the two nobles be banished. This is Mowbray's response.

It is most likely that Mowbray did have Gloucester murdered on Richard's direct orders and that Richard cancels the combat to avoid embarrassment.

---

3 *dearer merit* better reward
   maim wound
6 *these forty years* (In fact he was probably thirty-three in 1398. I see no reason why you couldn't change it to 'thirty'.)
8 *my tongue's use* (i.e. for speaking English)
9 *viol* stringed instrument played with a bow
10 *cunning* cleverly constructed
   cased up shut away
12 *knows no touch* doesn't know how to (play)
14 *portcullised* shut in (a portcullis is a heavy metal grating fortifying a gateway)
17 *fawn upon a nurse* start learning (a new language)

Act 1, Scene 3
Mowbray –

1	A heavy sentence, my most sovereign liege,
	And all unlooked-for from your highness' mouth.
	A dearer merit, not so deep a maim
	As to be cast forth in the common air,
5	Have I deservèd at your highness' hands.
	The language I have learnt these forty years,
	My native English, now I must forgo;
	And now my tongue's use is to me no more
	Than an unstringèd viol or a harp,
10	Or like a cunning instrument cased up –
	Or, being open, put into his hands
	That knows no touch to tune the harmony.
	Within my mouth you have enjailed my tongue,
	Doubly portcullised with my teeth and lips;
15	And dull, unfeeling, barren ignorance
	Is made my jailer to attend on me.
	I am too old to fawn upon a nurse,
	Too far in years to be a pupil now.
	What is thy sentence then but speechless death,
20	Which robs my tongue from breathing native breath?

Richard II

Henry Bolingbroke, Duke of Hereford

Henry Bolingbroke, Duke of Hereford (and later King Henry IV) 1366–1413) was son of John of Gaunt, Duke of Lancaster, and cousin to Richard II. At the beginning of the play Bolingbroke accuses Thomas Mowbray, Duke of Norfolk, of – amongst other things – murdering King Richard's (also Bolingbroke's) uncle, the Duke of Gloucester. Mowbray protests his innocence and demands trial by combat with Bolingbroke. Richard stops the combat just before it begins and orders that the two nobles be banished. (It is most likely that Mowbray did have Gloucester murdered on Richard's direct orders and that Richard cancels the combat to avoid embarrassment. Bolingbroke very probably knew of Richard's involvement.) Whilst in exile Bolingbroke's father (Old Gaunt) dies and Richard confiscates the family wealth in order to pay for his campaign in Ireland; he leaves another uncle, the Duke of York, in charge whilst he is away. Then Bolingbroke returns to England, with an army, and is challenged by York, who castigates him for breaking his banishment and 'braving arms against thy sovereign'. This is Bolingbroke's response.

Whilst Bolingbroke may seem to have 'right' on his side, there are many other indications that he is an ambitious and sometimes unscrupulous political schemer, with his sights on the crown. He is in his early thirties at this point.

---

2 *for Lancaster* to assume the title and rights of the Dukedom of Lancaster
4 *indifferent* impartial
8 *royalties* rights granted by the King
9 *perforce* by force
10 *unthrifts* spendthrifts (such as the King's favourites)
13 *kinsman* (This is 'cousin' in some editions, which was Aumerle and Bolingbroke's actual relationship; also both were cousin to Richard.)
16 *rouse* expose (literally, 'frighten from the lair' – as in hunting)
    chase them to the bay pursue them to the end ('bay' means 'last stand' in hunting)
17 *to sue my livery* the right to pursue my rights (i.e. to the inheritance which Richard had seized)
19 *distrained* seized (by crown officers)
18 *letters patents* official documents granting his title
20 *and all* and everything else
22 *challenge law* demand my rights
24 *of free descent* (i.e. free from any obstacle)

Richard II

Act 2, Scene 3
Bolingbroke –

1   As I was banished, I was banished Hereford;
But as I come, I come for Lancaster.
And, noble uncle, I beseech your grace,
Look on my wrongs with an indifferent eye.
5   You are my father, for methinks in you
I see old Gaunt alive. O then, my father,
Will you permit that I shall stand condemned
A wandering vagabond, my rights and royalties
Plucked from my arms perforce, and given away
10   To upstart unthrifts? Wherefore was I born?
If that my cousin king be King in England,
It must be granted I am Duke of Lancaster.
You have a son, Aumerle my noble kinsman;
Had you first died and he been thus trod down,
15   He should have found his uncle Gaunt a father
To rouse his wrongs and chase them to the bay.
I am denied to sue my livery here,
And yet my letters patents give me leave.
My father's goods are all distrained and sold,
20   And these and all are all amiss employed.
What would you have me do? I am a subject,
And I challenge law; attorneys are denied me,
And therefore personally I lay my claim
24   To my inheritance of free descent.

Richard III

Scrivener

The Scrivener is a clerk whose job is to make formal written copies of documents like this 'indictment' against Lord Hastings. (Hastings has assisted Richard in his machinations, but stops at the point when Richard was about to seize the crown.) He can be almost any age you would like him to be.

This tantalising little scene is his only one in the play and we know nothing else about this minor official. Is he 'bold' enough to protest at this 'palpable device'? Or will he play safe in amongst all this corruption and let what he knows remain securely locked up 'in thought'?

---

1   *indictment* formal document containing the accusation of a crime
2   *set hand* a formal handwriting (used in legal documents)
    fairly is engrossed is beautifully transcribed
4   *sequel* result (of my hard work)
5 & 8 *Eleven hours... five hours* (i.e. Hastings was executed six hours before the due processes of the law, starting with this document, are put into action)
6   *Catesby* (i.e. Sir William Catesby, a follower of Richard III)
7   *precedent* the original (from which he made his copy)
9   *Untainted* Not (even) formally accused
10 *the while* at this time
    gross stupid
11 *palpable device* obvious contrivance
12 *who's* (This is simply 'who' in some editions.)
    sees it not (i.e. 'not' as a 'contrivance')
14 *seen in thought* observed but not mentioned

80

Act 3, Scene 6
Scrivener –

Enter a Scrivener with a paper in his hand

1   Here is the indictment of the good Lord Hastings,
Which in a set hand fairly is engrossed,
That it may be today read o'er in Paul's –
And mark how well the sequel hangs together.
5   Eleven hours I have spent to write it over,
For yesternight by Catesby was it sent me;
The precedent was full as long a-doing;
And yet, within these five hours, Hastings lived,
Untainted, unexamined, free, at liberty.
10   Here's a good world the while! Who is so gross
That cannot see this palpable device?
Yet who's so bold but says he sees it not?
Bad is the world, and all will come to naught,
14   When such ill dealing must be seen in thought.   *Exit*

Richard III

Henry Stafford, Duke of Buckingham

Henry Stafford, Duke of Buckingham (1455–1483) was the confidant and most important supporter of Richard, Duke of Gloucester (later to become Richard III). King Edward IV (Richard's elder brother) has recently died; his son, Edward V, is only twelve and Richard is created Lord Protector until the boy reaches adulthood. Richard wants the crown and uses the loyal Buckingham in his campaign of propaganda and murder towards that end. Here Buckingham is describing to his master a public meeting he went to whose object was to try to drum up popular support for Richard's claims. He was about twenty-eight at this point.

I have cut some lines in order to create a better length for audition, and I have also made other minor modifications.

-----

2   *mum* silent
5   *tyranny for trifles* harshness towards trivial offences
7   *Duke* (i.e. Richard Plantaganet, Duke of York, 1412–1460)
9   *right idea* very image
10 *face* (This is 'form' in some editions.)
11 *victories in Scotland* (Richard had commanded the army that invaded Scotland the year before.)
12 *discipline in war* military prowess
15 *slightly handled* passed over lightly
16 *grew* (This is 'drew' in some editions. I prefer 'grew' because it leads to the climax of his oratory at line 18.)
20 *statuas* statues
25 *the Recorder* (i.e. the Recorder of London, a magistrate with both criminal and civil jurisdiction)
27 *inferred* alleged
28 *in warrant from himself* on his own behalf
32 *the vantage of* my opportunity from

Act 3, Scene 7
Buckingham –

1   Now, by the holy mother of our Lord,
       The citizens are mum, say not a word.
       I touched the bastardy of Edward's children,
       Th' insatiate greediness of his desire,
5   His tyranny for trifles, his own bastardy –
       As being got your father then in France,
       And his resemblance, being not like the Duke.
       Withal, I did infer your lineaments –
       Being the right idea of your father
10   Both in your face and nobleness of mind;
       Laid open all your victories in Scotland,
       Your discipline in war, wisdom in peace,
       Your bounty, virtue, fair humility –
       Indeed, left nothing fitting for your purpose
15   Untouched or slightly handled in discourse.
       And when mine oratory grew toward end,
       I bid them that did love their country's good
       Cry 'God save Richard, England's royal King!'
       But, so God help me, they spake not a word,
20   But, like dumb statuas or breathing stones,
       Stared each on other and looked deadly pale –
       Which, when I saw, I reprehended them,
       And asked the Mayor, what meant this wilful silence.
       His answer was, the people were not used
25   To be spoke to but by the Recorder.
       Then he was urged to tell my tale again:
       'Thus saith the Duke, thus hath the Duke inferred' –
       But nothing spoke in warrant from himself.
       When he had done, some followers of mine own,
30   At lower end of the hall, hurled up their caps,
       And some ten voices cried 'God save King Richard!'
       And thus I took the vantage of those few:
       'Thanks, gentle citizens and friends', quoth I;
       'This general applause and cheerful shout
35   Argues your wisdoms and your love to Richard' –
       And even here brake off and came away.

Richard III

Sir James Tyrrel

Sir James Tyrrel (c. 1450–1502) was Richard III's Master of Horse. In the previous scene Richard has asked Tyrrel to murder the sons of the late king, Edward IV, held in the Tower. Although Richard has put it about that they are illegitimate, he still fears a revolt to reinstate the eldest boy (Edward V) to the throne. Tyrrel agrees and gets two professional murderers (Dighton and Forrest) to help. These are his thoughts immediately after the deed.

Historically, we do not know whether he was responsible or not; he was executed in 1502 on completely unrelated charges. He was about forty-three at this point.

There are a number of detailed variations in words between different editions.

———————————

2 *arch* heinous
4 *Dighton and Forrest* (i.e. Myles Forrest... 'a fellow... bred in murder' and John Dighton... 'a big broad square and strong knave.' – from Sir Thomas More's *The History of King Richard III*)
6 *fleshed* hardened
8 *in their deaths' sad story* in telling the story of their (the princes') deaths
9 *babes* (They were in fact 11 and 13 at the time, i.e. 1483)
11 *alabaster* (i.e. white, like a figure on a tomb)
18 *replenished* complete
19 *prime* first
20 *both* (i.e. Dighton and Forrest)
    gone overwhelmed

Act 4, Scene 3
Tyrrel –

Enter Sir James Tyrrel
1   The tyrannous and bloody act is done;
     The most arch deed of piteous massacre
     That ever yet this land was guilty of.
     Dighton and Forrest, whom I did suborn
5   To do this piece of ruthless butchery –
     Albeit they were fleshed villains, bloody dogs –
     Melted with tenderness and mild compassion,
     Wept like two children in their deaths' sad story.
     'O thus', quoth Dighton, 'lay the gentle babes';
10   'Thus, thus', quoth Forrest, 'girdling one another
     Within their alabaster innocent arms;
     Their lips were four red roses on a stalk,
     And in their summer beauty kissed each other.
     A book of prayers on their pillow lay,
15   Which once', quoth Forrest, 'almost changed my mind;
     But O, the devil' – there the villain stopped,
     When Dighton thus told on, 'We smotherèd
     The most replenishèd sweet work of nature,
     That from the prime creation e'er she framed.'
20   Hence both are gone, with conscience and remorse.
     They could not speak, and so I left them both,
     To bear this tidings to the bloody king.
     Enter King Richard
23   And here he comes. All health, my sovereign lord!

Richard III

Henry Stafford, Duke of Buckingham

Henry Stafford, Duke of Buckingham (1455–1483) was Richard III's confidant and most important supporter. Earlier in the play he is a devious politician of great service to Richard in his ambitions for the throne (see the beginning of Act 3, Scene 5 for his description of his 'stratagems'). However, when Richard gains the throne, he proposes the killing of the young Prince of Wales and his brother ('Edward's children'). Buckingham is somewhat evasive and requests 'some little breath... before I positively speak in this' and leaves. A little later he returns and asks Richard for the earldom he had promised him – the implication (never stated) is that Buckingham will agree to kill the young princes in return. It's Richard's turn to be evasive – he has already organised someone else to carry out the killings – and he leaves saying, 'Thou troublest me; I am not in the vein'. Buckingham realises that he has to 'be gone... while my fearful head is on'. He raises an army in rebellion but is quickly captured. He was about twenty-eight at this point.

Shakespeare has Buckingham's execution take place shortly before the battle of Bosworth where Richard was killed.

I have cut the Sheriff's brief response between lines 10 and 11 and Buckingham's comment on 'Margaret's curse' between lines 21 and 22, to make the speech more succinct and less reliant on a knowledge of the whole play.

---

1   *Hastings* (an ally of Richard's executed earlier)
  Edward's children (sons of Edward IV – 'the Princes in the Tower')
  Gray and Rivers (son (by a previous marriage) and brother of Edward IV's wife, Elizabeth)
2   *King Henry and thy fair son Edward* (Henry VI and his son – NB not Edward IV)
3   *Vaughan* (another ally of Edward IV's wife, Elizabeth)
  miscarrièd perished
5   *discontented* unavenged
8   *All-Souls Day* (annual day of prayer for souls in purgatory – November 1st)
10–12 *This ... allies* (In Act 2, Scene 3 he says to Queen Elizabeth, 'Whenever Buckingham doth turn his hate / Upon your grace... God punish me / With hate in those where I expect most love.')
11 *fall on* (i.e. in revenge)
16 *determined respite* appointed (by God) time for the postponed punishment
17 *high All-Seer* (i.e. God)
  dallied trifled
19 *given in earnest what I begged in jest* (i.e. his earlier promise to Queen Elizabeth)
20 *He* (i.e. God)

Act 5, Scene 1
Buckingham –

*Enter the Duke of Buckingham with halberdiers, led by a Sheriff
to execution*

1   Hastings, and Edward's children, Gray and Rivers,
Holy King Henry and thy fair son Edward,
Vaughan, and all that have miscarrièd
By underhand, corrupted, foul injustice:
5   If that your moody, discontented souls
Do through the clouds behold this present hour,
Even for revenge mock my destruction!
This is All-Souls' day, fellow, is it not?
Why then All-Souls' day is my body's doomsday.
10   This is the day which, in King Edward's time,
I wished might fall on me, when I was found
False to his children and his wife's allies.
This is the day wherein I wished to fall
By the false faith of him whom most I trusted.
15   This, this All-Souls' day to my fearful soul
Is the determined respite of my wrongs.
That high All-Seer which I dallied with
Hath turned my feignèd prayer on my head,
And given in earnest what I begged in jest.
20   Thus doth He force the swords of wicked men
To turn their own points in their masters' bosoms.
Come lead me, officers, to the block of shame.
23   Wrong hath but wrong, and blame the due of blame.
                                    Exeunt Buckingham with officers

The Taming of the Shrew

Biondello

Biondello is a servant to Lucentio, a suitor to Bianca who is the sister of Katherina ('The Shrew'). It is not long before the planned wedding between Katherina and Petruchio. Biondello has just seen the bridegroom.

He can be almost any age you like.

2–3 *boots that have been candle-cases* boots so old that they have been used to keep candle-ends in
5 *chapeless* without a sheath (The 'chape' was the metal plate at the tip of the scabbard.)
  points tagged laces (used for fastening the hose to the doublet)
  hipped lamed in the hip
7–8 *glanders* and *mose in the chine* (both horse diseases; with swelling beneath the jaw and, in the final stage, suffering a dark discharge from the nostrils)
8 *lampass* (a horse disease: the fleshy lining behind the front teeth swells and hinders eating)
9 *fashions* farcy (a horse-disease similar to 'glanders')
  windgalls soft tumours on a horse's legs
  sped with the spavins far gone with swellings of the leg-joints
  rayed illuminated with
10 *yellows* jaundice
  fives strangles (swellings at the base of the ear)
  stark spoiled with absolutely wrecked by
11 *staggers* (horse-disease causing a staggering gait)
  begnawn with the bots gnawed at by intestinal worms
  weighed (This is 'swayed' in some editions.)
12 *shoulder-shotten* with a dislocated shoulder
  near-legged before with knock-kneed front legs
12–13 *half-cheeked bit* broken bit (the 'cheeks' are the rings attaching the bit to the bridle)
13 *headstall* (part of the bridle over the horse's head)
  sheep's leather (i.e. leather of inferior quality)
14 *restrained* drawn tight
15 *new-repaired* (This is 'now repaired' in some editions.)
16 *pieced* mended
  crupper strap (normally leather, passing under the horse's tail and stopping the saddle slipping)
18 *pack-thread* string

Act 3, Scene 2
Biondello –

1   Why, Petruchio is coming in a new hat and an old jerkin; a
       pair of old breeches thrice-turned; a pair of boots that have
       been candle-cases, one buckled, another laced; an old rusty
       sword ta'en out of the town armoury, with a broken hilt
5   and chapeless; with two broken points; his horse hipped,
       with an old mothy saddle and stirrups of no kindred;
       besides, possessed with the glanders and like to mose in
       the chine, troubled with the lampass, infected with the
       fashions, full of windgalls, sped with spavins, rayed with
10   the yellows, past cure of the fives, stark spoiled with the
       staggers, begnawn with the bots, weighed in the back and
       shoulder-shotten, near-legged before and with a half-
       cheeked bit and a headstall of sheep's leather which, being
       restrained to keep him from stumbling, hath been often
15   burst and new-repaired with knots; one girth six times
       pieced, and a woman's crupper of velour which hath two
       letters for her name fairly set down in studs, and here and
18   there pieced with pack-thread.

The Tempest

Ariel

Ariel is an airy sprite – invisible to all but the magician, Prospero, who rules the island (the setting of the play) and controls everybody and everything on it. Ariel's chief job is to carry out Prospero's wishes and is here describing how he (or 'she' or 'it') contrived the wreck of the ship containing Prospero's enemies whilst ensuring that no-one was harmed.

Ariel obviously enjoys this work – indeed, Prospero is very aware that in having all this fun Ariel might go too far in the heat of the moment. Ariel's moods go up and down quite violently – a bit like a child's. The success of this mission brings a high which switches to a violent low not long after this when Prospero says that there is more to do before his (or 'her' or 'its') promised freedom. Ariel, the magical being, has very human feelings.

Ariel can be played by either a man or a woman.

This speech is constructed from three shorter ones. It is also quite long and you could finish it at '... devils are here' (line18) or '... this sad knot' (line 25), but I've seen the whole speech done very excitingly and it certainly didn't feel too long.

---

1   *beak* prow (think of a bird's beak leading the way)

2   *waist* amidships (the fattest section of an Elizabethan ship)

5   *boresprit* bowsprit (Some editions have 'bowsprit', but I prefer *boresprit* as it gives a great feel for a ship boring through the waves.)
    flame distinctly make myself distinct flames in these different places

6–8 *Jove's lightnings... were not.* God's lightning-bolts, that precede the great claps of thunder, weren't as good as my efforts. (Some editors prefer *lightning* (singular) but I prefer the plural as it gives the idea of multiple flashes.)

16 *up-staring* standing on end

19 *sustaining garments* (There was a belief that clothes could keep you buoyant in water – probably born out of incidences of air getting trapped by certain clothing materials, thus – like a balloon – creating some buoyancy. Or perhaps Ariel is saying that even their clothes were left undamaged, as well as their bodies. You have to make up your own mind.)

25 *this sad knot* all miserable and huddled up (possibly imitated by Ariel)

28 *still-vexed Bermoothes* (Bermoothes (the 'es' is pronounced: 'ez') is roughly the Spanish for Bermudas, which were first colonised around the time *The Tempest* was written. These islands have a very stormy climate – hence 'still-vexed'.)

30 *charm... suffered labour* spell to calm them after the hell they just been through (probably all part of what Prospero told him to do)

33 *flote* sea

35 *wracked* wrecked (Some editors have 'wrecked', but I prefer the 'a' – it's more evocative of the state of the ship and those in it.)

The Tempest

Act 1, Scene 2
Ariel –

1   I boarded the King's ship. Now on the beak,
     Now in the waist, the deck, in every cabin
     I flamed amazement. Sometimes I'd divide,
     And burn in many places. On the topmast,
5   The yards, and boresprit would I flame distinctly,
     Then meet and join. Jove's lightnings, the precursors
     O' th' dreadful thunderclaps, more momentary
     And sight-outrunning were not. The fire and cracks
     Of sulphurous roaring the most mighty Neptune
10   Seem to besiege, and make his bold waves tremble,
     Yea his dread trident shake. Not a soul
     But felt a fever of the mad, and played
     Some tricks of desperation. All but mariners
     Plunged in the foaming brine, and quit the vessel,
15   Then all afire with me. The King's son Ferdinand,
     With hair up-staring – then like reeds not hair –
     Was the first man that leaped; cried, 'Hell is empty,
     And all the devils are here!' Not a hair perished.
     On their sustaining garments not a blemish,
20   But fresher than before; and as thou bad'st me,
     In troops I have dispersed them 'bout the isle.
     The King's son have I landed by himself,
     Whom I left cooling of the air with sighs
     In an odd angle of the isle, and sitting,
25   His arms in this sad knot. Safely in harbour
     Is the King's ship, in the deep nook where once
     Thou called'st me up at midnight to fetch dew
     From the still-vexed Bermoothes, there she's hid;
     The mariners all under hatches stowed,
30   Who, with a charm joined to their suffered labour,
     I have left asleep. And for the rest o' th' fleet,
     Which I dispersed, they have all met again,
     And are upon the Mediterranean flote
     Bound sadly home for Naples,
35   Supposing that they saw the King's ship wracked,
     And his great person perish.

The Tempest

Caliban

Caliban is the offspring of the witch Sycorax and an unnamed devil. He is the 'savage and deformed slave' of the magician Prospero, who was exiled to the island twelve years beforehand. Initially, (before the play) Prospero and his daughter Miranda treated Caliban kindly and tried to teach him 'civilised' values, but everything changed when Caliban attempted to rape her. And, by the start of the play he is being treated brutally like a slave and he fights back at every turn.

Caliban's parentage and all that Prospero and Miranda say about him make him appear the lowest of beings (his name could be an anagram of 'Cannibal' in its seventeenth-century spelling with only one 'n'); but through his own mouth comes some extraordinarily beautiful language revealing a very sensitive mind. He is often played as a monster but I don't believe he should be played as a grotesque; he is like the native American Indians discovered not long before Shakespeare wrote the play: lacking a complete understanding of the values of 'civilised western society', and falling foul of it.

Prospero has just called him, 'What, ho! Slave, Caliban! / Thou earth, thou, speak!'

This is several speeches put together. You could cut line 6, but I rather like the 'bridge' it creates between the two parts of the speech.

----

2 *wicked* harmful
3 *fen* mildew
4 *south-west* (Thought to bring pestilence.)
18 *sty* confine (like a pig)
22 *red plague* (A type of plague which produced red sores.)
     rid destroy

Act 1, Scene 2
Caliban –

1   [*Within*] There's wood enough within.
      Enter Caliban
      As wicked dew as e'er my mother brushed
      With raven's feather from unwholesome fen
      Drop on you both! A south-west blow on ye
5   And blister you all o'er!
      I must eat my dinner.
      This island's mine, by Sycorax my mother,
      Which thou tak'st from me. When thou cam'st first,
      Thou strok'st me and made much of me, wouldst give me
10   Water with berries in 't, and teach me how
      To name the bigger light, and how the less,
      That burn by day and night. And then I loved thee,
      And showed thee all the qualities o' th' isle,
      The fresh springs, brine-pits, barren place and fertile –
15   Cursed be I that did so! All the charms
      Of Sycorax, toads, beetles, bats, light on you!
      For I am all the subjects that you have,
      Which first was mine own king, and here you sty me
      In this hard rock, whiles you do keep from me
20   The rest o' th' island.
      You taught me language, and my profit on 't
      Is I know how to curse. The red plague rid you
23   For learning me your language!

The Tempest

Caliban

Caliban is the offspring of the witch Sycorax and an unnamed devil. He is the 'savage and deformed slave' of the magician Prospero, who was exiled to the island twelve years beforehand. Initially, (before the play) Prospero and his daughter Miranda treated Caliban kindly and tried to teach him 'civilised' values, but everything changed when Caliban attempted to rape her. And, by the start of the play he is being treated brutally like a slave and he fights back at every turn.

Caliban's parentage and all that Prospero and Miranda say about him make him appear the lowest of beings (his name could be an anagram of 'Cannibal' in its seventeenth-century spelling with only one 'n'); but through his own mouth comes some extraordinarily beautiful language revealing a very sensitive mind. He is often played as a monster but I don't believe he should be played as a grotesque; he is like the native American Indians discovered not long before Shakespeare wrote the play: lacking a complete understanding of the values of 'civilised western society', and falling foul of it.

Caliban has met up with Stephano and Trinculo, who were ship-wrecked on the island at the beginning of the play. After initial suspicion, Caliban, warmed by the wine they've given him, swears his allegiance to them, instead of Prospero. In their next scene together he tells them how Prospero 'stole' the island from him and in revenge he asks the two men to kill his former master. He then describes how they might accomplish the deed.

This is several speeches put together.

---

2   *paunch* stab (him) in the belly
5   *weasand* wind-pipe
7   *sot* fool
9   *but* only
10 *brave utensils* fine household furnishings
14 *nonpareil* without equal (in beauty)
19 *brave brood* many healthy children

Act 3, Scene 2
Caliban –

1   Why, as I told thee, 'tis a custom with him
     I' th' afternoon to sleep. There thou mayst brain him,
     Having first seized his books; or with a log
     Batter his skull, or paunch him with a stake,
5   Or cut his weasand with thy knife. Remember
     First to possess his books, for without them
     He's but a sot as I am, nor hath not
     One spirit to command – they all do hate him
     As rootedly as I. Burn but his books.
10   He has brave utensils, for so he calls them,
     Which when he has a house he'll deck withal.
     And that most deeply to consider is
     The beauty of his daughter. He himself
     Calls her a nonpareil. I never saw a woman
15   But only Sycorax my dam and she,
     But she as far surpasseth Sycorax
     As great'st does least.
     She will become thy bed, I warrant,
     And bring thee forth brave brood.
20   Within this half hour will he be asleep.
     Wilt thou destroy him then?

Titus Andronicus

Marcus Andronicus

Marcus Andronicus is a Roman tribune and brother to Titus Andronicus, a Roman general. Marcus is a good, reasonable and caring politician who spends the play advocating what is best for people; he is the voice of sanity in amongst all the corruption, chaos and carnage of the play. He speaks later of his 'frosty signs and chaps of age, / Grave witnesses of true experience' indicating that he's probably over forty; but I think he could be played in his thirties.

At this point, whilst out hunting, he has just come across his niece Lavinia (Titus' daughter) in a piteous state. It may seem extraordinary that he can speak like this to her – she has been raped, her hands cut off and tongue cut out – but, remember that people invariably react unexpectedly in extreme circumstances.

In the play the complete speech is nearly double this length – far too long for audition unless around five minutes' worth is specifically required.

----

2   *Cousin* (often used for a close relative outside the immediate family)
3   *would all my wealth would wake me!* I would give everything to be woken!
16   *Tereus* (In mythology, Tereus rapes his wife's sister, Philomela, and cuts out her tongue to keep her quiet. Shakespeare uses much of the rest of this story through the play.)
17   *defect* expose
21   *Titan* (god of the sun)
22   *to be encountered with* when he encounters
24   *thy heart* what is in your mind (As well as the root of emotions, the heart was believed to be the origin of thoughts.)
25   *rail at* abuse

Act 2, Scene 4
Marcus –

Enter Marcus from hunting to Lavinia
1   Who is this? My niece, that flies away so fast?
     Cousin, a word: where is your husband?
     If I do dream, would all my wealth would wake me!
     If I do wake, some planet strike me down,
5   That I may slumber an eternal sleep!
     Speak, gentle niece: what stern ungentle hands
     Hath lopped and hewed and made thy body bare
     Of her two branches, those sweet ornaments,
     Whose circling shadows kings have sought to sleep in,
10   And might not gain so great a happiness
     As half thy love? Why dost not speak to me?
     Alas, a crimson river of warm blood,
     Like to a bubbling fountain stirred with wind,
     Doth rise and fall between thy rosèd lips,
15   Coming and going with thy honey breath.
     But sure some Tereus hath deflowered thee,
     And, lest thou shouldst detect him, cut thy tongue.
     Ah, now thou turn'st away thy face for shame;
     And notwithstanding all this loss of blood,
20   As from a conduit with three issuing spouts,
     Yet do thy cheeks look red as Titan's face,
     Blushing to be encountered with a cloud.
     Shall I speak for thee? Shall I say 'tis so?
     O that I knew thy heart, and knew the beast,
25   That I might rail at him to ease my mind!

Titus Andronicus

Marcus Andronicus

Marcus Andronicus is a Roman tribune and brother to Titus Andronicus, a Roman general. Marcus is a good, reasonable and caring politician who spends the play advocating what is best for people; he is the voice of sanity in amongst all the corruption, chaos and carnage of the play. He speaks here of his 'frosty signs and chaps of age, / Grave witnesses of true experience' indicating that he's probably over forty; but I think he could be played in his thirties.

At this point, four of the principal protagonists have just been killed (all within twenty lines), thus resolving the central conflicts of the play. Marcus (with Titus' remaining son, Lucius) seizes the moment to address those remaining with this plea for sanity.

---

5   *mutual* unified (i.e. working co-operatively together)
7   (From this line on, the rest of the speech is assigned to another character in some editions.)
    bane poison
11 *frosty signs* white hairs
    chaps of age wrinkles
13 *attend* pay attention to
14 *erst* once
    our ancestor (i.e. Aeneas, the father of the legendary founder of Rome, Romulus)
14–18 (Aeneas, a Trojan, escaped the destruction of Troy and on his subsequent travels met Dido, Queen of Carthage.)
19 *Sinon* (the traitor who persuaded the Trojans to admit the wooden horse)
20 *the fatal engine* the wooden horse
21 *civil wound* wound inflicted by civil war
22 *compact* made of

Act 5, Scene 3
Marcus –

1   You sad-faced men, people and sons of Rome,
      By uproars severed, as a flight of fowl
      Scattered by winds and high tempestuous gusts,
      O, let me teach you how to knit again
5   This scattered corn into one mutual sheaf,
      These broken limbs again into one body;
      Lest Rome herself be bane unto herself,
      And she whom mighty kingdoms curtsy to,
      Like a forlorn and desperate castaway,
10   Do shameful execution on herself.
      But if my frosty signs and chaps of age,
      Grave witnesses of true experience,
      Cannot induce you to attend my words,
      [*To Lucius*] Speak, Rome's dear friend, as erst our ancestor,
15   When with his solemn tongue he did discourse
      To lovesick Dido's sad attending ear
      The story of that baleful burning night
      When subtle Greeks surprised King Priam's Troy.
      Tell us what Sinon hath bewitched our ears,
20   Or who hath brought the fatal engine in
      That gives our Troy, our Rome, the civil wound.
      My heart is not compact of flint nor steel,
      Nor can I utter all our bitter grief,
      But floods of tears will drown my oratory
25   And break my utt'rance even in the time
      When it should move ye to attend me most,
      And force you to commiseration.
      Here's Rome's young captain; let him tell the tale,
29   While I stand by and weep to hear him speak.

Titus Andronicus

Saturninus

Saturninus is elected Emperor through the support of Titus Andronicus (a victorious Roman general), but turns against him, fearing his popularity, and becomes an accessory to the plots against Titus led by his Empress, Tamora. (Although he is ignorant of many of her darker deeds.)

Titus' daughter, Lavinia, is raped and mutilated (and her husband, also Saturninus' brother, murdered); two of Titus' sons are (falsely) accused of these crimes and Saturninus sentences them to death. Titus agrees to pay a ransom for his sons' lives – his severed hand – only to be be delivered shortly afterwards of their severed heads. He swears vengeance. Seemingly mad, he gets his family to fire arrows bearing messages to the gods asking for justice – these land in Saturninus' palace courtyard.

Saturninus is completely dedicated to his own selfish ends with no thought of a monarch's duty to his subjects. We are given no proper indication of his age, but I think he could be quite young , because of his ignorance of so much of what is really going on.

———————————

2   *overborne* oppressed

3   *extent* exercise

4   *egal* equal (From the French '*égal*' – this is spelt 'egall' in some editions.)

8   *even with law* that which is lawful

9   *and* (This is 'an' in some editions.)

11   *wreaks* vengeful acts

18   *blazoning* proclaiming

19   *humour* whim

21   *ecstasies* insanity

24 & 25   *he* (This is 'she' (i.e. justice) in some editions, but I prefer the directness of 'he' (i.e. Saturninus).)

25   *He'll* Titus will

     awake arouse

     he (i.e. Saturninus)

Act 4, Scene 4
Saturninus –

*Enter Saturninus, the Emperor, and Tamora, the Empress, with
her two sons, and attendants. The Emperor brings the arrows in
his hand that Titus shot at him*

1   Why, lords, what wrongs are these! Was ever seen
    An emperor in Rome thus overborne,
    Troubled, confronted thus; and for the extent
    Of egal justice used in such contempt?
5   My lords, you know, as know the mightful gods,
    However these disturbers of our peace
    Buzz in the people's ears, there naught hath passed
    But even with law against the wilful sons
    Of old Andronicus. And what and if
10 His sorrows have so overwhelmed his wits?
    Shall we be thus afflicted in his wreaks,
    His fits, his frenzy, and his bitterness?
    And now he writes to heaven for his redress.
    See, here's to Jove and this to Mercury,
15 This to Apollo, this to the god of war –
    Sweet scrolls to fly about the streets of Rome!
    What's this but libelling against the senate
    And blazoning our unjustice everywhere?
    A goodly humour, is it not, my lords? –
20 As who would say, in Rome no justice were.
    But, if I live, his feignèd ecstasies
    Shall be no shelter to these outrages;
    But he and his shall know that justice lives
    In Saturninus' health, whom if he sleep,
25 He'll so awake as he in fury shall
    Cut off the proud'st conspirator that lives.

Troilus and Cressida

Troilus

Troilus is the son of King Priam of Troy during the pointless and inter-minable siege of that city. He is insanely in love with Cressida, daughter of Chalchas, who has defected to the Greeks. Her uncle, Pandarus (now effectively her guardian) knows of Troilus' feelings for her and, in this scene, he has been baiting him with talk of her beauty. The enflamed Troilus hits back with this speech.

In many ways he is a typical romantic hero, both in loving Cressida and advocating the rightness of continuing of the war with the Greeks. However, he becomes victim (in both love and war) to his naïveté.

---

4   *endrenched* drowned (This is 'indrenched' in some editions.)
8   *Handlest* (You) touch upon
     that her hand that hand of hers
10 *to* compared with
     seizure clasp
12 *spirit of sense* the very essence of the feeling of touch
15 *balm* ointment

Act 1, Scene 1
Troilus –

1   O Pandarus! I tell thee, Pandarus –
     When I do tell thee 'There my hopes lie drowned',
     Reply not in how many fathoms deep
     They lie endrenched. I tell thee I am mad
5   In Cressid's love; thou answer'st 'She is fair',
     Pour'st in the open ulcer of my heart
     Her eyes, her hair, her cheek, her gait, her voice;
     Handlest in thy discourse – O, that her hand,
     In whose comparison all whites are ink
10   Writing their own reproach, to whose soft seizure
     The cygnet's down is harsh, and spirit of sense
     Hard as the palm of ploughman. This thou tell'st me –
     As true thou tell'st me – when I say I love her.
     But saying thus, instead of oil and balm
15   Thou lay'st in every gash that love hath given me
     The knife that made it.

Troilus and Cressida

Ulysses

Ulysses is one of the Greek commanders during the pointless and interminable siege of Troy. Early in the play he is the voice of sanity amongst the fractious Greek leaders ground down by the continuing stalemate of the siege. This scene starts with Agamemnon, the Greek general, trying to encourage the other commanders by saying that their seven year long failure to conquer is a test imposed by Jove. He is followed by the long-winded Nestor trotting out platitudes. Then Ulysses seizes the moment to tell them what's really wrong with the Greek army: it's moral weakness and lack of respect for 'degree', i.e. a strict ordering to ensure the best functioning army (and society).

In mythology he is better known by his Greek name, Odysseus, and is a principal character in Homer's *Iliad*, then the central figure in the *Odyssey*, which recounts his long series of adventures after the Trojan war. He is generally thought of as being early middle-aged, but I don't see why he couldn't be in his twenties.

I have used the latter half of the (very long) speech as it is in the play.

----

2   *melts* (This is 'meets' in some editions – I prefer 'melts' because it helps set up his description of an ugly, messy decay that follows.)

3   *mere oppugnancy* total conflict

4   *should* would (and at lines 6, 7, 8 and 10)

5   *sop* formless mess (literally, bread or toast soaked in wine or water)

6   *Strength should be lord of imbecility* The (physically) strong would rule the (physically) weak

7   *rude* brutal

9   *jar* conflict

11   *everything includes itself in power* each thing embraces mere power (i.e. without responsibility)

12   *will* (merely) self-willed

     appetite (merely) greed

20   *in* (This is 'with' in some editions.)

20–21 *in a purpose / It hath* when it wants

24   *Exampled by* Learned from (by example)

24   *pace* action

29   *lives* (This is 'stands' in some editions.)

Act 1, Scene 3
Ulysses –

1	Take but degree away, untune that string,
	And hark what discord follows. Each thing melts
	In mere oppugnancy. The bounded waters
	Should lift their bosoms higher than the shores
5	And make a sop of all this solid globe;
	Strength should be lord of imbecility,
	And the rude son should strike his father dead.
	Force should be right; or rather, right and wrong –
	Between whose endless jar justice resides –
10	Should lose their names, and so should justice too.
	Then everything includes itself in power,
	Power into will, will into appetite;
	And appetite, an universal wolf,
	So doubly seconded with will and power,
15	Must make perforce an universal prey,
	And last eat up himself. Great Agamemnon,
	This chaos, when degree is suffocate,
	Follows the choking.
	And this neglection of degree it is
20	That by a pace goes backward in a purpose
	It hath to climb. The general's disdained
	By him one step below; he, by the next;
	That next, by him beneath. So every step,
	Exampled by the first pace that is sick
25	Of his superior, grows to an envious fever
	Of pale and bloodless emulation.
	And 'tis this fever that keeps Troy on foot,
	Not her own sinews. To end a tale of length:
29	Troy in our weakness lives, not in her strength.

The Two Gentlemen of Verona

Speed

Speed is page to Valentine, one of the 'Two Gentlemen'. He is cheeky and impertinent, and has just been teasing his master about his infatuation with Silvia, daughter of the Duke of Milan. Valentine is so besotted with her that he doesn't realise that he's being sent up by Speed, until the servant decides to diagnose his master's condition in this speech.

'I know you are in love' (line 1) is taken from Valentine's previous line to make sense of the speech in isolation.

He is usually played in his twenties, but I don't see why he couldn't be played older.

------

2   *Sir* (A courtesy title, often bandied around in this play.)
       wreathe fold
2–3   *like a malcontent* one dissatisfied
3   *relish* sing (with pleasure)
5   *ABC* reading-primer
6   *grandam* grandmother
       takes diet is dieting for health purposes
7   *watch* lie awake
       puling whiningly
8   *Hallowmas* All Saints' Day (or All-Hallows – 1st November – traditionally a day on which paupers received special alms)
9–10 *the lions* (The lions kept at the Tower of London or the heraldic lions on the royal standard.)
10   *presently* immediately
11   *want* lack
12   *metamorphosed* transformed
       with by

Act 2, Scene 1
Speed –

1   Marry, I know you are in love by these special marks: first,
you have learned, like Sir Proteus, to wreathe your arms, like
a malcontent; to relish a love-song, like a robin-redbreast; to
walk alone, like one that had the pestilence; to sigh, like a
5   schoolboy that had lost his ABC; to weep, like a young wench
that had buried her grandam; to fast, like one that takes diet;
to watch, like one that fears robbing; to speak puling, like a
beggar at Hallowmas. You were wont, when you laughed, to
crow like a cock; when you walked, to walk like one of the
10   lions; when you fasted, it was presently after dinner; when
you looked sadly, it was for want of money. And now you are
metamorphosed with a mistress, that when I look on you I
13   can hardly think you my master.

The Two Gentlemen of Verona

Proteus

Proteus is one of the 'Two Gentlemen'. Initially, he seems completely in love with Julia. His father, Antonio, decides that he must go to join his friend, Valentine (the other 'Gentleman'), in the court of the Duke of Milan to be 'tried and tutored in the world'. Proteus and Julia exchange rings and he vows to remain faithful whilst he is away. Meanwhile, Valentine has fallen in love with the Duke's daughter, Silvia, and they plan to elope. Proteus arrives, meets her and is immediately besotted himself. Valentine unaware of this complication asks Proteus to help in the elopement and then leaves to make his own preparations. Proteus, left on his own, confesses his new love and ponders the consequences.

He could be anywhere between late teens and late twenties.

---

1 *heat* passion
15, 16 *advice* knowledge
18 *picture* outward appearance
21 *no reason but* no doubt that
23 *compass* win

Act 2, Scene 4
Proteus –

1	Even as one heat another heat expels,
	Or as one nail by strength drives out another,
	So the remembrance of my former love
	Is by a newer object quite forgotten.
5	Is it mine eye, or Valentine's praise,
	Her true perfection, or my false transgression,
	That makes me reasonless to reason thus?
	She is fair, and so is Julia that I love –
	That I did love, for now my love is thawed,
10	Which like a waxen image 'gainst a fire
	Bears no impression of the thing it was.
	Methinks my zeal to Valentine is cold,
	And that I love him not as I was wont.
	O, but I love his lady too-too much,
15	And that's the reason I love him so little.
	How shall I dote on her with more advice,
	That thus without advice begin to love her?
	'Tis but her picture I have yet beheld,
	And that hath dazzlèd my reason's light.
20	But when I look on her perfections
	There is no reason but I shall be blind.
	If I can check my erring love, I will;
23	If not, to compass her I'll use my skill. *Exit*

The Two Gentlemen of Verona

Valentine

Valentine is one of the 'Two Gentlemen'. He and Silvia, the daughter of the Duke of Milan, are in love, but his so-called friend Proteus (the other 'Gentleman') attempts to steal her. Proteus engineers Valentine's banishment. While Valentine is travelling he is captured by outlaws, who invite him to be their leader because he claims to have 'killed a man' and is educated. He accepts providing that they don't attack defenceless women or the poor. At this point he is waiting for them to return from a mission.

Valentine may seem like a somewhat gullible romantic leading man, but he is resourceful. He lies to the outlaws and later is quick to rescue Silvia when she is about to be raped and strongly threatens another rival suitor to her. He could be anywhere between late teens and late twenties.

---

1   *use* custom
2   *shadowy desert* deserted place shaded by trees
3   *brook* cope with
5   *nightingale's complaining notes* (In mythology Tereus raped Philomela who was turned into a nightingale which, when remembering Tereus's crime, sang with its breast pressed against a thorn.)
6   *record* sing
12   *cherish* treat kindly
     swain lover
14   *my mates* (i.e. the outlaws)
15   *Have* Who have
     passenger traveller

Act 5, Scene 4
Valentine –

Enter Valentine

1   How use doth breed a habit in a man!
This shadowy desert, unfrequented woods
I better brook than flourishing peopled towns.
Here can I sit alone, unseen of any,
5   And to the nightingale's complaining notes
Tune my distresses and record my woes.
O thou that dost inhabit in my breast,
Leave not the mansion so long tenantless
Lest, growing ruinous, the building fall
10   And leave no memory of what it was.
Repair me with thy presence, Silvia;
Thou gentle nymph, cherish thy forlorn swain.
Noises within
What hallooing and what stir is this today?
These are my mates, that make their wills their law,
15   Have some unhappy passenger in chase.
They love me well; yet I have much to do
To keep them from uncivil outrages.
18   Withdraw thee, Valentine. Who's this comes here?
He stands aside

The Two Noble Kinsmen

Gerald

Gerald (or Geraldo) is a pedantic schoolmaster, who enjoys taking charge and showing off his (self-perceived) command of language (especially in line 1). He doesn't appear in any other scene, and is only briefly mentioned earlier (in Act 2, Scene 3) as 'the dainty dominie' (fussy schoolmaster) in sole charge of organising an entertainment at the court of Duke Theseus.

He is probably the creation of John Fletcher and not Shakespeare, but very few people will worry about this for an audition.

He could be any age above mid-twenties.

Some editions have this speech as prose, not verse.

---

2 *tediosity* tediousness
  disinsanity utter folly
3 *rudiments* basic principles (for the entertainment they are about to perform)
5 *by a figure* to use a figure of speech (Also in line 15, but not line 20)
5–6 *the very plum-broth / And marrow of my understanding* the very richest qualities and core of my intellect ('Plum-broth' was an exotic mixture of dried fruit, meat and spices, often eaten at Christmas, and 'marrow' means core)
8 *coarse frieze capacities* crude, limited intelligence (*Frieze* is a rough woollen cloth.)
  jean judgements simple minds ('jean' is a cheap cotton cloth – as in today's 'jeans')
11 *Proh deum, medius fidius* O God, so Heaven help me!
12 *Forwhy* So (this is how it should work)
13 *Close* Hidden
15 *hums* murmurs approval
16 *go forward* continue (to address him)
18 *Meleager* (A mythical Greek hero who slew a boar, which had been sent to ravage the country. The implication is that they should do it well.)
19 *Break comely out* Burst out (from hiding) in a graceful fashion
  lovers loving subjects (of Duke Theseus)
20 *Cast yourselves in a body decently* Arrange yourselves properly (for the dance)
21 *by a figure* in (dance) formation
  trace and turn go through your steps and turns

Act 3, Scene 5
Gerald –

Enter Gerald and Countrymen attired as Morris dancers

1   Fie, fie,
What tediosity and disinsanity
Is here among ye! Have my rudiments
Been laboured so long with ye, milked unto ye,
5   And, by a figure, even the very plum-broth
And marrow of my understanding laid upon ye?
And do you still cry 'Where?' and 'How?' and 'Wherefore?'
You most coarse frieze capacities, ye jean judgements,
Have I said, 'Thus let be', and 'There let be',
10   And 'Then let be', and no man understand me?
Proh deum, medius fidius – ye are all dunces!
Forwhy, here stand I; here the Duke comes; there are you,
Close in the thicket. The Duke appears; I meet him,
And unto him I utter learnèd things
15   And many figures. He hears, and nods, and hums,
And then cries, 'Rare!', and I go forward. At length
I fling my cap up – mark there! Then do you,
As once did Meleager and the boar,
Break comely out before him. Like true lovers,
20   Cast yourselves in a body decently,
And sweetly, by a figure, trace and turn, boys.

The Winter's Tale

Leontes

Leontes is the King of Sicilia and husband of Hermione. Polixenes, King of Bohemia and his friend since childhood, has been staying at his court for nine months. He has just announced that he must return home tomorrow. Leontes suggests that he stay another week, and at first Polixenes refuses but Hermione manages persuade him. However, in the course of their discussion, Leontes perceives an undue intimacy between them and becomes suddenly extremely jealous, convinced that they have been having an affair. He cannot hide how upset he is but does not say why; instead he says he will walk with his son, Mamillius. Hermione says that she and Polixenes will go into the garden and has just asked if he'll join them. This is his response.

From his demeanour Mamillius is probably about seven; he was born when his father was twenty-three, so Leontes is probably about thirty.

---

5   *the neb* her mouth (to be kissed)
    the bill the announcement (of her, supposed, feelings for Polixenes)
7   *allowing* approving
    To her allowing husband Towards her husband, who licenses such behaviour
8   *a forked one* (1) cuckolded (himself), (2) deceitful (Hermione)
11 *Contempt and clamour* An outburst of contemptuous laughter
18 *Sir Smile* (i.e. Polixenes smiling – with deceit)
19 *Whiles* As long as
21 *revolted* unfaithful
23 *bawdy planet* destructive influence
24 *Where 'tis predominant* Whenever it's in the ascendant (i.e. has a strong influence)
    Think it Be assured of it
26 *No barricado for a belly* There is no way of barricading a womb
    Know 't Be certain that
28 *on 's* of us

Act 1, Scene 2
Leontes –

1   To your own bents dispose you; you'll be found,
     Be you beneath the sky. [*Aside*] I am angling now,
     Though you perceive me not how I give line.
     Go to, go to!
5   How she holds up the neb, the bill to him,
     And arms her with the boldness of a wife
     To her allowing husband! [*Exeunt Polixenes and Hermione*]
         Gone already.
     Inch-thick, knee-deep, o'er head and ears a forked one!
     Go play, boy, play. Thy mother plays, and I
10   Play too; but so disgraced a part, whose issue
     Will hiss me to my grave. Contempt and clamour
     Will be my knell. Go play, boy, play. There have been,
     Or I am much deceived, cuckolds ere now,
     And many a man there is, even at this present,
15   Now, while I speak this, holds his wife by th' arm,
     That little thinks she has been sluiced in 's absence,
     And his pond fished by his next neighbour, by
     Sir Smile, his neighbour. Nay, there's comfort in 't,
     Whiles other men have gates, and those gates opened,
20   As mine, against their will. Should all despair
     That have revolted wives, the tenth of mankind
     Would hang themselves. Physic for 't there's none.
     It is a bawdy planet, that will strike
     Where 'tis predominant; and 'tis powerful. Think it:
25   From east, west, north, and south, be it concluded,
     No barricado for a belly. Know 't,
     It will let in and out the enemy
     With bag and baggage. Many thousand on 's
29   Have the disease and feel 't not. – How now, boy?

The Winter's Tale

Antigonus

Antigonus is a nobleman at the court of King Leontes of Sicilia, and married to Paulina. With his wife he defends Queen Hermione against the King's accusation of her supposed adultery with King Polixenes of Bohemia. However, when it comes to the crunch, Paulina is far stronger than Antigonus. She confronts Leontes with Hermione's new-born daughter (as yet, unnamed), but the King rejects the baby claiming that she must be a result of the adultery and should be 'consumed with fire'. Antigonus, and other lords protest; Leontes relents, on condition that Antigonus swears to 'bear it to some remote and desert place... where chance may nurse or end it'. Here, Antigonus, with the baby, has just stepped ashore in remote Bohemia.

He is usually thought of as middle-aged, but (in Act 2, Scene 1) he talks of his three daughters, aged eleven, nine and five – by normal Elizabethan standards, this would place him in his late twenties or early thirties.

In fact, Hermione is not dead; but Antigonus and the audience think she is until near the end of the play.

I have cut seven lines from this speech to make it a better length for audition.

---

16 *Perdita* (i.e. The lost one)
19 *toys* (i.e. of no value)
20 *superstitiously* against accepted beliefs
21 *squared* directed
27 *thy character* the written account of you (proving her identity)
   these (i.e. gold, jewels, etc., found later)
28 *both breed thee, pretty* both be enough for your upbringing, pretty one
29 *And still rest thine* And still leave enough for your future
36 *savage clamour* (i.e. the growls of the advancing bear)
37 *chase* hunt (i.e. he sees the bear)

Act 3, Scene 3

Antigonus –

1   Come, poor babe.
    I have heard, but not believed, the spirits o' th' dead
    May walk again. If such thing be, thy mother
    Appeared to me last night, for ne'er was dream
5   So like a waking. To me, in pure white robes
    Like very sanctity, she did approach
    My cabin where I lay; thrice bowed before me,
    And, gasping to begin some speech, her eyes
    Became two spouts. The fury spent, anon
10 Did this break from her: 'Good Antigonus,
    Since fate, against thy better disposition,
    Hath made thy person for the thrower-out
    Of my poor babe according to thine oath,
    Places remote enough are in Bohemia:
15 There weep, and leave it crying; and for the babe
    Is counted lost for ever, Perdita
    I prithee call it.' Affrighted much,
    I did in time collect myself, and thought
    This was so, and no slumber. Dreams are toys:
20 Yet for this once, yea superstitiously,
    I will be squared by this. I do believe
    Hermione hath suffered death, and that
    Apollo would – this being indeed the issue
    Of King Polixenes – it should here be laid,
25 Either for life or death, upon the earth
    Of its right father. Blossom, speed thee well! [*He lays down
        the babe and a scroll*]
    There lie, and there thy character. [*He lays down a box*] There
        these,
    Which may, if fortune please, both breed thee, pretty,
    And still rest thine. [*Thunder*] The storm begins. Poor wretch,
30 That for thy mother's fault art thus exposed
    To loss and what may follow! Weep I cannot,
    But my heart bleeds, and most accursed am I
    To be by oath enjoined to this. Farewell.
    The day frowns more and more. Thou'rt like to have
35 A lullaby too rough; I never saw
    The heavens so dim by day. A savage clamour!
    Well may I get aboard. This is the chase.
38 I am gone for ever!   *Exit, pursued by a bear*

117

The Winter's Tale

Autolycus

Autolycus is a petty thief and con. man with a great zest for life. When we first see him in the previous scene he picks the pocket of the Clown, a likeable and somewhat stupid rustic. Autolycus next appears earlier in this (long) scene, disguised as a peddler, at the sheep-shearing festival. There he entertains the crowds, singing songs, selling trinkets, and picking pockets. As the festivities continue he finds further opportunities for theft until the jollities are suddenly curtailed. He is here on his own reflecting on his successes.

He could be any age you care to make him.

———————

3   *trumpery* worthless goods
      stone gem
4   *table-book* note-book
5   *horn-ring* (These were supposed to have magic properties.)
      fasting being empty
7   *hallowed* sacred
      benediction blessing
8   *best in picture* best looking (i.e. fullest and easiest for picking)
10   *wants but something* short of only one thing
12   *pettitoes* feet (literally, pigs' trotters)
13–14 *stuck in ears* completely concentrated on listening
14   *placket* petticoat (or the slit in a petticoat, the sense is what lies beyond)
15   *geld a codpiece of a purse* cut off a purse from a codpiece (Men would tie their purses to their codpieces.)
      could (This is 'would' in some editions.)
17   *my sir's* (i.e. the Clown's)
      nothing triviality
18   *cut* (i.e. cutting the purse as at line 15)
18–19 *festival purses* (i.e. full of money to spend)
19   *hubbub* (This is 'whoo-bub' in some editions.)
21   *choughs* jackdaws (i.e. his victims)

118

Act 4, Scene 4
Autolycus –

Enter Autolycus

1   Ha, ha, what a fool honesty is! And trust, his sworn
brother, a very simple gentleman! I have sold all my
trumpery; not a counterfeit stone, not a ribbon, glass,
pomander, brooch, table-book, ballad, knife, tape, glove,
5   shoe-tie, bracelet, horn-ring to keep my pack from fasting.
They throng who should buy first, as if my trinkets had
been hallowed, and brought a benediction to the buyer; by
which means I saw whose purse was best in picture; and
what I saw, to my good use I remembered. My clown, who
10   wants but something to be a reasonable man, grew so in
love with the wenches' song that he would not stir his
pettitoes till he had both tune and words, which so drew
the rest of the herd to me that all their other senses stuck in
ears. You might have pinched a placket, it was senseless.
15   'Twas nothing to geld a codpiece of a purse. I could have
filed keys off that hung in chains. No hearing, no feeling
but my sir's song, and admiring the nothing of it. So that in
this time of lethargy I picked and cut most of their festival
purses, and had not the old man come in with a hubbub
20   against his daughter and the King's son, and scared my
choughs from the chaff, I had not left a purse alive in the
22   whole army.

Bibliography

The Plays

I referred to the Arden, New Penguin, Oxford, Peter Alexander and Riverside editions and found different aspects to recommend each of them. However, if I'm to recommend one particular edition – for actors – I would marginally recommend the Oxford editions. *The Complete Works* (General Editors: Stanley Wells & Gary Taylor) were published in 1988 by Oxford University Press, and about half of the individual plays have appeared in paperback with some excellent notes. The remaining plays are 'forthcoming'.

Shakespeare Reference

Charles Boyce, *Shakespeare – The Essential Reference to His Plays, His Poems, His Life, And More* (Roundtable Press)

Peter Quennell and Hamish Johnson, *Who's Who in Shakespeare* (Routledge, 1996)

Gareth and Barbara Lloyd Evans, *Everyman's Companion to Shakespeare* (Dent, 1978)

About Shakespeare and His Plays

There are an impossible number of books on this subject; the ones I've got most out of are:

Anthony Burgess, *Shakespeare* (Penguin, 1970) – this not a history book but a wonderful evocation of who Shakespeare might have been and how he might had lived his life.

A. L. Rowse, *Shakespeare the Elizabethan* (Weidenfeld & Nicholson, 1977) – although written by an eminent academic historian, this is a good read.

F. E. Halliday, *Shakespeare In His Age* (Duckworth, 1971) – a much more detailed account, involving more of the other important personalities of the age.

Jan Kott, *Shakespeare Our Contemporary* – although he writes about only a few of the plays, the author gives a wonderful evocation of Shakespeare in our time.

About Acting

Uta Hagen, *A Challenge for the Actor* (Macmillan, 1991) – the best book on acting ever written.

Simon Dunmore, *An Actor's Guide to Getting Work* (A. & C. Black, 1996) – all you need to know about auditioning and all aspects of being an actor.